Becoming Who We Need To Be

Colin Wright

Thank you very much if you purchased this book (or supported your local library by borrowing it there): I appreciate you.

Even if you acquired it by some more nefarious means, though, I hope you find some value in it. Consider passing that value-windfall on by being especially kind today :)

Library of Congress Cataloging-In-Publication Data
Becoming Who We Need To Be / Colin Wright — 2nd ed.
ISBN: 978-1-68287-009-9
eISBN: 978-1-68287-008-2

1. Philosophy. 2. Self-Help. 3. Essays. 4. Personal Growth.
5. Communication.

Cover design by Colin Wright

For Josh and Ryan.

In any free society, the conflict between social conformity and individual liberty is permanent, unresolvable, and necessary.

—*Kathleen Norris*

Teach one individual today and a society would get taught tomorrow.

—*Hermann J. Steinherr*

Contents

Introduction

This is a book about the challenges we face as individuals and as societies, and becoming who we need to be to face them.

We are living through a fortunate moment in human history. It's not the first of such moments, nor will it be the last, hopefully. But enviable though it may be, ours is also a time of great upset and uproar, and no small amount of uncertainty.

This uncertainty, though uncomfortable, can be a positive thing. It means the possibilities are so many and varied that we as individuals might have trouble sorting the relevant ones from those we can safely ignore, or ignore for now. It means we're developing rapidly in fields ranging from microprocessors to microbiota, from material science to the materiality of the universe.

Living today is like being stuck in a cyclone filled with hundred dollar bills and cinnamon rolls: it's a safe bet we'll be happy when the winds subside, but at the moment we're mostly confused as hell and worried about paper cuts and frosting in our hair.

Attempting to sit this out, to avoid the cyclone and its benefits and downsides, is unlikely to shield us from its impact. This swirl of events, this confusing chaos composed of innovations and news items and social movements and international volatility is not going to slow down, but in fact speed up. It won't shrink to a manageable size if we wait just out of range; it will expand to encompass even those currently calm in sideline seats where some panicked people have sought refuge.

This seemingly novel craziness is the result of relatively recent shifts in how we think, how we communicate, and the technologies we've developed. These deviations have iteratively, and at times revolutionarily, changed the pace and power of the slow-moving flow forward that we've always experienced, but the rhythm is an upbeat riff on more of the same. We've always experienced change, we just haven't always experienced it at this pace and intensity.

We each have a choice to make, today, about how we deal with the knowledge that change isn't going away, and that it will in all likelihood continue to pick up steam as it progresses.

Frictions that have long stood in the way of progress have become fuel; toeholds rather than barriers. We can either scream into the wind and denounce the whole exercise, decry it as unfair and not right and something we won't take part in because it's new and different and scary, or we can learn to make the currents work for us and affect the change we'd like to see in the world. We can hide our heads in the sand or we can take responsibility for what happens next.

One of the better ways to understand complex systems, I've found, is to understand the context in which they exist and function.

It's a relatively simple exercise to learn a few facts about the state of the computing industry, but it's another thing altogether to understand why it's evolving in the way it is, and where it might go next. Environmental pressures might emerge simultaneously from the smartphone industry, the world of video games, and from the military, while the confluence of these factors shapes what the next generation of microprocessors are capable of. The business model of this industry determines how and where they're produced, while the politics that underpin sprawling multinational corporations and border-based national bureaucratic systems help us understand the concrete realities shaping the spaces in which these synthetic brains are born.

I initially considered writing this book as a single long narrative, each piece connecting to each other, starting with something like the self-help industry and ending with a discussion of meta-reality, with hundreds of other important points touched on in between, each stop serving as connective tissue, and the whole sprawling mess demonstrating that none of these topics exist in isolation. The concept of belief is inextricably connected to artificial intelligence, just as "truth" in the realm of politics is intertwined with the metrics we use to define our personal success.

This method would have worked in a way, I think, because these pieces are intertwined if you trace the threads between them carefully enough. But the connections make more of a web than a braided cord, and they would be tricky to spin together in a linear fashion suitable for presentation in this format. That in mind, I've instead opted to group ideas together into broader topics of discussion, which allows me to point out isolated pieces of the web and how they connect with one another, before moving on to other parts of the pattern.

It's important to note from the beginning that there's no way for me to touch on every topic in each of these areas, nor is it possible to address all the connections or all the relevant data. These are intended to be foundational starting points—context to understand the broad strokes of an industry, a moment in history, or a realm of thought—upon which to build. They are in no way the final word on anything at all, and will be most ideally treated as jumping off points for further learning and thinking and exploring.

I'll be asking many questions, and offering few answers. In some cases I'll present multiple, mutually exclusive answers, all possibly true to someone, or in some situations. But I think you'll find the questions are often the more valuable asset. Answers are generally the end of a conversation, while questions are the beginning of one. If we can ask the right questions, we can begin moving in the right direction. That journey is what I hope to instigate here, not any particular conclusion or rigid set of beliefs. If you finish a chapter having attained some new information to mull over, or a new point of view from which to consider a topic, you're doing it right.

Many of the concepts in this book are presented because they represent challenges we face, as societies and as individuals, in the coming years. It's important to remember that a challenge needn't be taxing or miserable. A challenge can be a testing ground for our ideas—again, collectively and as singular human beings—and can liberate us to separate the useful from the well-regarded but ultimately pointless or harmful. Challenges allow us to test our own mettle and appraise our infrastructural sturdiness. Challenges inspire action and incentivize us to focus on what's important. Another word for "challenge" is "opportunity."

We have the opportunity to become the people we've always hoped to be: the most refined, well-developed versions of ourselves possible.

We have the opportunity to build societies, and communities of societies, that help us grow and become greater as a species. To organize in ways that allow us to face the tenacious intellectual antagonists that have limited us since the first spark of sentience. We have the opportunity to see what we're collectively capable of.

The first step in taking advantage of a malleable situation, a period in which everything is in flux and ripe for reworking, is to understand as completely as possible what's happening. What is it that we're even looking at and feeling? What variables are in play both within us and within our societies?

Let's explore that context.

Let's figure out what we might accomplish.

Context

We never truly understand something until we understand the context in which it exists.

The context around a news item, for instance, consists of the circumstances that shape the setting of the news item, the personalities involved and how they're connected to what's being reported on, the rationale for why this news item is occurring and why it's occurring in the way that it is, the meaning of the words being used within the news item, and the secondary bits of information one must know to fully understand what's happening.

Context, in short, is the big picture. The big, sprawling, picture. And we require an unobstructed view of this big picture if we're to follow what's happening in the world and within our own lives, and if we're to form relevant opinions.

Context is also, very unfortunately, often left out of the reporting of the news, conversations about anything, and even our internal thought processes which shape how we see the world.

Let's start small, with journalism, and work our way up to how our brains operate.

Journalists as individuals are generally not to blame for the lack of complete context around a topic they're covering. Providing complete context, I would argue, would require an article the size of every bit of information we've ever collected. To pinpoint the absolute, perfect coordinates of a newspaper piece about a driver intentionally running down cyclists with his car in Southern California, for instance, you'd need to be able to place that bit of information onto a metaphorical map containing all information connected in any way to that specific event, and then extend outward, reporting all bits that connect to those bits, layer upon layer. Eventually, you'd find yourself explaining fluid dynamics in the local Community section of the paper, and though that would no doubt be an educational experience, it wouldn't be a very convenient way to get your information. Especially if you're just looking to understand the bare-basics of what's happening in the world around you.

So what journalists and journalism entities do, instead, is triangulate. They have this piece about maniac car drivers and victimized cyclists, and they attach it to a few other relevant pieces of information they assume will be the most likely to help an otherwise uninformed reader understand why this piece of news is important. That means a local beat reporter would write up a piece that tells the factual details of the incident—a man has been swerving his SUV into cyclists he encounters on the road, causing them to crash, to become injured—and then she includes some information about local road safety organizations that have been trying to get bike lanes installed, references another recent article about how local funds have been mismanaged by a seemingly corrupt Treasurer, and mentions three other incidents of road rage in nearby towns, in which drivers took out their frustration about having to share the road with cyclists on the cyclists themselves.

By most measurements, this is a proper news article. It

gives us what we need to know about a particular thing, triangulates where that bit of news falls within the larger scope of news being reported, and does it, as much as possible, in an unsalted, fact-first way.

But something has happened to this model over the last few decades. Newspapers primarily depend on selling advertisements to stay in the black. They can't afford to report the news, online or in print, if they can't get people to buy ads on their websites and in their papers. They can't sell sufficient ads, or charge enough for each ad placed, if their readership numbers aren't sufficiently high. Very often this works on a "cost per *mille*" (CPM) model, which means "cost per thousand" readers. They earn more per ad for each thousand readers, because that means more people seeing that ad. This is a simple model that's worked decently well for a long time, but which is not without its downsides.

Click-bait is a type of article presented on the web, or potentially in a newspaper, which primarily exists to attract eyeballs, not to inform. An old school publishing motto for pushing news you know will get people buying papers can be summed up as, "if it bleeds, it leads." Meaning if it's sensational, if it's gory, if it's sexy or salacious in some way, put that above the fold on the front page. That sensationalist story will attract more readers, those readers will count toward our CPM, and we'll earn more money, which allows us to keep the doors open.

A lot of news networks justify the use of click-bait in all its manifestations by pointing out that if they have more money in the bank, they can put more reporters on the ground. And this is absolutely true: if a paper or website can regularly pull in more readers and can sell out their ad space at high premiums, they're in a great position to hire the best writers and editors, to pay for longer-format pieces about important topics, and can spend more time clearing the way, legally and financially, so that real journalists can do their jobs and do them well.

But this, of course, isn't always what happens. Although there are examples of click-bait news organizations getting serious and spending an increasing amount of their ill-gotten gains on genuinely excellent journalism—*Buzzfeed's* politics and tech-sector work in 2016, after many years of nothing but celebrity gossip and sugary think pieces comes to mind—for every turnaround story in the right direction there are three crossing paths with them, going the other way. *Buzzfeed* may have repurposed a large chunk of their income toward high-quality reporting and multimedia work to accompany it, but the normally reliable *New York Times* has taken heat for repurposing some of its funding toward the empty-calorie work that shares well on Facebook while providing little new information or insight.

Also making the job of the modern journalist difficult is the fixation on bite-sized and easy-to-digest bits of news, ideally with a lot of images or videos of some kind. Research seems to show that people don't like to read, or don't like to read much, and are increasingly engaging with news on their smartphones while in-transit or between other activities. This reshaping of the news makes sense, then, especially if you're hoping to keep those readership numbers high. But this new shape is less ideal for in-depth reporting and made more for very superficial explanations about what's happening. If you only have 300 words with which to tell a reader why China's increasingly aggressive stance in the South China Sea is important, you have to bring very different skills to bear than you would in a long-form piece of a comparably luxurious 3,000 words.

It's not impossible to deliver value within such limitations. If you ever doubt our capacity to concisely and effectively communicate while confined, peruse the often brilliant work of writers who are operating on Twitter, limited to 140 characters. We are capable of expanding and contracting our ambitions based on the space allotted. But to be restricted in this way—confined to dozens of words, when the scope of the issue being discussed cannot even be displayed as raw numbers in that space—is too limiting and flawed to achieve the intended ends. You tweet on Twitter, you don't try to write an essay there. Likewise, you don't put a tweet on a two-page spread within a printed publication.

Presenting context properly in the news, then, will require that we present the right information in the right places, and then intuitively connect these pieces to each other.

One of the most fascinating and valuable pieces of property on the internet, in terms of pure utility, is Wikipedia. This oft-reviled resource is criticized for being riddled with errors, but in reality, if you look at the data, it's actually the most accurate encyclopedia ever made, weighing in at 99.5% accurate in studies conducted in the US and Europe. Wikipedia contains far more false facts and errors than any other encyclopedia ever made, too, because it's so much bigger than any traditional publication. Wikipedia is over 60 times larger than the next-largest encyclopedia, and spans nearly 5.4 million articles in English, alone, which add up to 2.9 billion words. At any given moment, Wikipedia is especially prone to abuse or bias, but these errors are also typically corrected quickly and reliably, while errors contained in more traditional encyclopedias, like *Britannica*, remain from edition to edition, lacking the crowdsourced effort that Wikipedia enjoys.

Wikipedia is a remarkable creature in part because it connects wildly diverse topics together into a mesh that, while not in any way near complete, represents one of the most thorough maps of knowledge that's ever existed in human history. You can start anywhere on Wikipedia and, by clicking highlighted words within the articles, end up on the other end of the epistemological map. There are resources online that allow you to choose any article on Wikipedia as a starting point and then calculate how many steps it takes, clicking on those links within the article, to get to the main page for Philosophy (97% of all articles on Wikipedia eventually lead back to Philosophy, as of February 2016). There's a game that propagated around the internet in 2009 called "Clicks to Jesus," which challenged players to see if they could get to the Wikipedia page for Jesus within five clicks from any random article they were assigned. A similar game, "Clicks to Hitler," also became quite popular.

These games are only possible because the connections between articles in Wikipedia are expansive, and demonstrate how incredibly diverse topics are related to one another. Is it funny that you can trace a link-path between the Third Punic War and Jesus in just five steps? Yes. Is it also highly illustrative of how interconnected seemingly unconnected topics are, and how relevant oft-ignored subject matter might be in understanding something quite relevant in your own life? Yes.

What I'd love to see is a mechanism for connecting resources provided by news entities that works something like Wikipedia's system of connective tissue links, though with more timely focus and professional fact-checking. Some networks are already attempting something along this vein: *Vox*, an explainer site, built their current website around the concept of information cards, each of which contains a relevant chunk of context that can be reshuffled, sorted, and dealt out when necessary for new pieces that require them. *The New York Times* and other large, traditional publications have been experimenting with this as well, dynamically injecting modular, reusable content into new articles. They've pre-built, say, a short brief about China's history with the

Nine-Dash Line and why it's relevant to the South China Sea so that it can be included alongside or within any new pieces written about that or related subjects.

I don't know that there will be a more thorough example of networked information than Wikipedia any time soon, but it would certainly be helpful. The economics of journalism can't be ignored, and while I disagree with the assertion that there's no way to fund high-quality work except to invest time and resources in low-quality work, I do understand the drive to do so. Hopefully they'll be able to create more thorough, expansive, interconnected infrastructure in the meantime, whether using cards or modular chunks of information, which will allow them to present a more complete context for their stories. It's an imperfect solution, but far better than being forced to cram the news equivalent of *Moby Dick* into a column the size of a baseball card.

Data by itself isn't as valuable as data provided with context. You can hand me a chart full of numbers, but lacking an understanding of what these numbers represent, this chart will be worthless to me. Given the context in which it exists, however—a list of upcoming lottery picks, or the nuclear codes for a country's arsenal—the numbers may become very valuable, indeed.

Context without reliable data isn't valuable, either. You can give me a book that relates the events leading up to the American Civil War, but if the book says the war happened in 1487 (it didn't) and took place between the Inca and the Maori (it didn't) and was fought to determine which group knew the best dances (it wasn't, but that would have been neat), then that book isn't particularly useful to me. Except, perhaps, for its entertainment value.

The combination of access to reliable information and having that information presented within a larger context is valuable because it tells us not just what is, but also why, and how, and as a consequence of what, and what might happen next.

Without access and context, we can only deliver empty words or lackluster, heartfelt but misguided opinions. And unfortunately, that could accurately describe many of our conversations.

We're not required to provide bibliographies for our conversations with friends and family. We're not required to cite our sources while tipsily holding court over which political party is the right one, or when expressing our opinion about international trade partnerships while out on a date.

And it's a good thing that we don't thoroughly bibliographize, because that would probably become tiresome pretty quickly. Your drinking buddies wouldn't show up for the next happy hour, and your chances of a second date would dissipate.

That said, we don't always hold ourselves to the highest of standards when it comes to conversations, and considering that a good deal of what we believe is derived from these interactions, it's unfortunate that we don't have a better mechanism for ensuring we're not reinforcing unbacked opinions or false facts, casually and probably unintentionally.

There's a chance that we'll have a technological solution to this problem in the near future. The emergence of on the fly voice-to-text translation software is one harbinger of what will likely become *in situ* fact-checking software, used first by news networks to quickly check the truthfulness of statements made by politicians and other figures, but eventually making its way to the consumer market, as well. This software is remarkable and already common in our homes, though it's more often used for other purposes: translation software, dictation apps, and even the voice-activated assistants made by Apple, Google, and Amazon.

You could leave this app open, the microphone turning on automatically when conversation begins. As you have your discussion, the app might chime in during moments of silence, correcting vague fictions or outright mistruths, and providing evidence to support its assertion. It could also provide additional information about the topics being discussed, and could do so visually, if you leave your device on the table between you and your discussion partner, or audibly, summing up the content of the links it provides and recommending additional topics worth discussing as offshoots from your current one.

This example is just one of the more obvious use-cases for such technologies, and in a way, it already exists—though currently it's not an automatic system with soft-AI backing it and it's only for online conversations rather than real-life discussions.

There are non-partisan fact-checking sites and apps all over the place these days, and though politicians and their parties are distrustful of anything that calls the honesty and integrity of their positions into question, the unbiased nature of most of these apps and sites is laudable, and the information they provide is easily applied and referenced. There's usually some kind of invented metric used to indicate how accurate or inaccurate a given statement is ("True" to "Pants-On-Fire," in the case of popular fact-checking website *Politifact*), alongside information supporting their assertions.

We are going to need more and more nuanced tools of this nature in the coming years. We're experiencing a credibility crisis when it comes to entities which were once considered infallible, but which we can now easily check, seeing for the first time the cracks in their facade.

We also find ourselves stuck inside fact bubbles which reinforce our existing ideologies, and which fail to provide us with full context, with complete, accurate information, and which leave us, as a result, holding worldviews that are not based on accurate representations of what's happening.

How we process data and context internally is just as vital as how we take it in. As such, it's a real problem when we lack the tools, time, or motivation to think critically.

Our brains are remarkable organs, and the more we learn about them, the more we understand about their full complexity and interconnectedness with the rest of our bodies, the more awestruck we are at our own amazingness.

And rightfully so. Our bodies, and the brain-parts of our bodies in particular, are damn cool. Worthy of awe. But if we fail to make proper use of them, these race cars we've got the keys to are kept in the garage, or driven at a snail's pace, or drunkenly smashed into oncoming traffic.

Our brains get sharper as we use them. They're shaped and fed by many things, including our health and general state of psychological wellness. But they're honed when exposed to challenges, frictions, and new data. Your brain can come up with answers to questions, but only if you know the words required to understand the question and present an answer, and only quickly and accurately if you've fed it a steady diet of other questions and information from which it can derive answers.

The fastest, most powerful computer in the world can't tell you what two plus two equals if it hasn't been given mathematical data to work with, leaving it ignorant of how numbers work and what "plus" means. Likewise, you may be blessed with a remarkably powerful brain, but it won't be put to practical use if you don't give it facts and conceptual information to start from.

We feed our brains in many ways.

Raw data intake is one of the most basic ways to amplify one's thinking capability. The more you learn, the more you know, and the more you know, the more you're capable of slamming together seemingly disparate bits of information to derive new knowledge.

Our brains reward us when we have "eureka" moments. The empirical data on this is still blurry—there are several theories about what's happening when clarity snaps into place, and many different parts of the brain activate at once to make it happen—but the feeling is familiar to anyone who's ever muddled through a problem, only to recognize a clear, now-obvious solution after a period of thought. It's a feeling that should also be familiar to anyone who's ever stepped away from a creative task to do something else, allowing that completely unrelated task to shake a new idea free.

One way to illustrate this process is based on a theory about how our brains store memories and information.

I picture everything I know as individual nodes in a great big web: each bit of information is a dot, and each dot of data is connected to other dots, those connections representing connections between those pieces of data. For example, the dot for "apple" would be connected to "red" and "fruit" and "sweet," but also to "gravity" and "flora" and "worm." That main "apple" concept would also be connected to other points based on personal memories and associations, not just factual data. Maybe it has strands reaching out toward "cut on my finger" because of that one time I sliced my pinky while cutting up apple slices, and "the feeling of eating apple slices and peanut butter with my girlfriend while watching a movie" because of a fond memory consisting of all the sensations from that specific moment in time, including those apple slices.

Each complete memory, then, is made up of its own bundle of points, and those points are clustered, but still attached to a million other points elsewhere, either contained in other memories, or learned through books, through conversations, or through experience.

To have a strong memory, then, is to be skilled at making connections between existing information within your brain-web, and to be capable of tracing those connections to find relevant information when you need it. So when you meet someone new, maybe you attach the name of that person to another person you've met who has the same name, or a historical figure who sounds similar. Perhaps you link their tiny nose to a portrait of a historical figure with a similarly small snout you saw at a museum, while also attaching this new acquaintance to the friend through whom you were introduced. Recollecting this person's name and face, then, is a simple matter of recalling one or more of those connections, then tracing it back to this person and their collection of points on the web.

"Thinking outside the box," in this sense would mean retreating from a well-explored bundle of nodes to go play in another subsection of your brain. While trying and failing to figure out what might be going wrong with the plumbing in your bathroom, you might step away from activities and thought processes that focus your attention on the portion of your mental web directly related to plumbing—pipes and engineering and tools and water properties—and instead listen to some music, watch some TV, or get coffee with a friend. Thinking outside the box, then, is really about refocusing on different parts of your mental web, and attacking a problem from a completely different angle. Instead of trying to come up with solutions that are already connected to your understanding of plumbing, you might come at it from knowledge and memories associated with music or apples or playing guitar. It may be that the solution is found, not within your current understanding of plumbing, but within your body of knowledge about how vibrations in strings create sound, and how that sound can be adjusted by knobs and tension.

Expanding our web—our collection of knowledge and memories—expands our internal sense of context. That means doing more and a wider variety of things, meeting a new and greater diversity of people, and acquiring new, diversified knowledge increases our ability to put new information and experiences into accurate context. This then helps us to understand what's happening and what needs to happen next.

There are many different theories about how the brain works and how we process information. It may be that we learn this web metaphor doesn't hold up under more intense scrutiny and some other imagery makes more sense. But as a visual for understanding why having access to more information and making connections between the bits of information we already have is important, it's a useful one.

We need to be capable of comparing the information and perspective that we have with that of other people. In order to combine the information we've collected in this way, we need to be capable of having valuable, productive discussions, rather than simply propagandizing at each other all the time.

In order to be capable of having such discussions, and to be a valuable part of such interactions, we as individuals need to be aware of the powerful tools we're born with, and how we might best utilize them. It's our choice whether we rev them up or leave them sitting in the garage, collecting dust. But if we want to make full use of these gifts that we have as living, thinking human beings, we must push ourselves to expand our horizons and seek out difficult, uncomfortable thoughts, rather than avoiding them and filling our days with reaffirmations and sugary falsehoods.

It's easier to create a pleasant, soft, cushy reality than to build one that's growth-oriented and fulfilling on a deeper, more complex level. Happiness is more predictably found as part of a lifestyle that involves consistent and interesting challenges than in one without discomfort, hurdles, and friction.

Language

The language we use—the words, the sentence structure, the patterns and rhythms—are important. They're icons that represent something, that have meaning. If they lose their meaning, or if that meaning becomes diluted, then we lose, to some degree, the powers that language grants us.

And what does language grant us? Why was it such an important development in our species' history?

Because language gives us the capacity to communicate data. It allows us to express concepts which are tangible and observable, but also those which are not.

Language allows us to say, "There's a deer right there, and it looks fast."

Language also allows us to say, "I bet we can catch that deer if we try."

And further, "If we catch the deer, we can eat it and grow strong."

And finally, "I wonder if that deer also desires to grow strong."

What we have is a stairstepping progression of shared awareness, from external to internal, which is the consequence of being able to explore ideas with each other, but also to slap a label on complex ideas for use in our own internal rumination.

We understand concepts before we have the words to describe them. When you're a baby, you eventually come to grasp what grass is, and you have sensory information about how it feels, how it smells, probably how it tastes, because you're a baby and want to taste everything, and all of this information combines in your brain to make you aware of this object in your environment.

Having a word to define such a thing, though, allows us to examine it more closely. Knowing the word "grass" makes it far more likely that we'll then look for other grasses or grass-like things in our world. If grass is a bed of prickly, green, plant-smelling things growing out of the ground, is that other thing over there grass? No, we learn, that's a tree. Okay, now we have multiple points of comparison. We have iconic versions of both of these objects in our brains, and we can continue to compare and contrast everything we encounter in terms of these objects we can concisely describe. We can use both grasses and trees as landmarks, and describe other things in terms of how they're similar or dissimilar to grasses and trees.

Lacking this ability to label, we'd be less capable of immediately comparing any new thing, any new experience, any new person, to those we've experienced before. Our brains work these comparisons lightning-fast, and a negative consequence of this is our propensity for bias and prejudice. If we've encountered data about a person or thing in the past that implies it might be dangerous, our knee-jerk reaction is to avoid that thing, or treat it as a threat.

That said, this quick-twitch labelling is largely a positive thing. It means we're capable of ambling around through the world, identifying characteristics of things we encounter, and using our past knowledge of other things with other characteristics to make educated guesses about what this completely novel, but not unknowable, thing might be. If it might be dangerous, if it might be edible, if it might be like us.

That's one value of language as it applies to our understanding of the world around us: without the iconography of words, we'd be less capable of comprehending novelty, and thinking complex thoughts.

One level up, language allows us to imagine. It allows us to think a step forward in time, taking what we know about deer, or what we know about creatures that are furry and which walk on four legs, and what we know about ourselves, and work that information into a story arc.

The value of this cannot be overstated. Many creatures have the ability to predict, in a way, what will happen based on past experience. They understand cause and effect in an instinctual way, which is what allows lab rats to be trained to respond to certain smells with panic because in the past that smell has indicated an imminent electric shock. It also allows cats to learn that if they paw at the cabinet door in just the right way, they usually get food in the near-future.

Some other animals, though, are capable of more complex manipulation of the present to impact the future. Some creatures, like magpies, dolphins, chimpanzees, and elephants, are able to compile knowledge about a particular aspect of their environment, and then think, "Well, what happens if I do this?" They're able to manipulate the world around them to achieve an imagined outcome.

In one oft-repeated instance of this, an elephant is shown a highly desired bit of food, but that food is placed high above its head, well out of reach. An array of different objects is present within the elephant's pen, and after some muddling about, and a great deal of looking back and forth at the food and then at the objects available, the elephant moves a sturdy plastic cube underneath where the food hangs. It then steps up onto the cube to increase its height, allowing it to reach up and snag the treat.

This is an example of tool usage, and it's incredibly rare within the non-human animal kingdom. There are perhaps a dozen species that we have confirmed will sometimes use tools, and this capacity almost always aligns with a sophisticated use of language: elephants use a complex sign language to organize societies and solve problems, while magpies and crows screech out meaningful noises at each other and members of their species living in different parts of the world have identifiable regional dialects.

We're still learning the full scope of non-human animal capabilities in this regard, but the human capacity for tool usage is immense. We became the dominant Earthly species through our manipulation of our environments, and that manipulation relies on our magnificent tools. The invention and construction of these tools required the same thing that the elephant required: the ability to recognize a problem, to take the problem apart, and then to imagine what might happen if we applied various solutions to that problem.

The elephant had to think, "If I use that stick, might I reach the food? Would it allow me to grab the food in some way? No, probably not. What about that cube? Can I move the cube? If I move it, can I stand on it? Will that give me sufficient height to reach the food? Perhaps." The elephant almost certainly didn't use those exact words, not speaking English (as far as we know), but it would have had to break apart the situation into pieces, mentally move those pieces around, imagine a future in which things are arranged differently, and then figure out how to make that future manifest.

This is what we do every time we hone a rock into an arrowhead or construct and program a particle accelerator. We're identifying and labelling the world around us, and then imagining how it could be if it was different. If those minerals were mined, refined, processed, reshaped, and put in a box, might they become pipes for use in the walls of a house? Imagine trying to invent indoor plumbing without language. We might make it part of the way, describing each component as a collection of sensory data. But being able to label components and what we might do with them, and being capable of describing the world we want to see, one with accessible toilets and pipes, allows us to work as individuals and groups to make that future a reality.

The next level up is being capable of imagining the meaning of a new set of circumstances. This is, as far as we know, something that only humans are capable of doing, but it's also something that's difficult to observe and measure for many reasons, so it's hard to say for certain. Did that dolphin rescue a drowning passenger from a capsized ship because they understood the meaning of such a gesture, or did they do it out of instinct or because of a misunderstanding of the situation? We're prone to anthropomorphizing and ascribing human motivations to such acts, at least in part because that's how and why we respond to things. We don't just see the pieces; we mentally put them together and derive meaning from them. It makes sense, then, that we would infer that other creatures do the same, whether or not they have the capacity to do so.

Make no mistake: this intellectual step is a crazily complex one, even though we take it for granted. When driving to work and stuck behind a vehicle driving slower than the speed limit, you ascribe meaning to that person's actions through the lens of what's called "attribution bias." If you're annoyed by their slow driving, that inferred meaning will probably not be generous to the other driver: they're a bad person, they're in the way, and they're doing this because they're stupid or incapable. That these assumptions about the situation are possibly incorrect—maybe they're driving slowly because they're in deep thought about elephant tool usage?—is irrelevant. Ascribing meaning to acts unto itself is impressive, even if we often fail to arrive at a correct, or fully correct, understanding of the situation.

We're able to do this because we're capable of understanding our environment in a deep way. Because we're able to compare and contrast ideas, hold an encyclopedia of these objects in our brains, and then expound upon those tangible things to come up with intangible possibilities. We think beyond the food and the box we might stand on to reach it. We think about ourselves, our own height and arm, we consider our fundamental, if not mathematical, understanding of gravity and physics, and what it will feel like to have the food, to taste the food, how the world will look once we have it.

The meta-context of meaning requires that all of these other understandings fall into place, first. Then it requires one more trick: the ability to apply a label to a feeling, to a state of being, to a desire, to an intention. For us to achieve a prediction about why that other driver is driving slowly requires that we're capable of labelling the physical world in which we and our cars exist, but also that we have the language to make predictions about this unknown person's reason for acting as they are. We need to be able to imagine and label their personal characteristics, gleaned from incredibly small amounts of data, and make assumptions as to what that information tells us about their ambitions, how they pursue those ambitions, and why.

This represents a stunningly complex sequence of logical leaps. And even when we're wrong, which we often are when it comes to making judgments from a distance with very limited information, that we're capable of juggling all these ideas and slapping them together into the outline of a scenario is only possible because we're able to encapsulate complex ideas like "rude" and "incompetent" and "driving" and "slow" using concise labels that we can string together into other, larger, even more wildly complex ideas. The larger ideas are compressed into phrases and sentences that we shape into exponentially larger concepts contained in sentences and paragraphs, which are themselves encoded and expressed as we mumble to ourselves about that stupid, rude, incompetent, slow driver who's keeping us from getting to work on time and who should learn to frickin' drive.

This level of thinking allows for meta-cognition—which means being aware of our own awareness, and thinking about ourselves thinking—which allows us to work together for larger, shared goals. It's also what allows us to feel existential angst, to worry and to wonder how things could have been. It's the ability to not just imagine how we might change the environment to achieve our ends, but what reality actually is, what is happening when we think, and further, what is happening when someone else thinks. What's going on in that deer's head, anyway? And should I eat something that thinks?

Many of our modern issues are the consequence of our high level of cognition. We've built a world in which we can grow intellectually because a large number of people are physically safe. This growth is positive in that it allows us to build things like computers and the internet, inventions that have resulted in intangible versions of reality but which seem quite real to those who use it. But it's also resulted in myriad psychological issues, from depression to post-traumatic stress disorder. Some of these issues have been with us for a long time—depression is often the result of a chemical imbalance, and is likely something our ancestors suffered from, as well, even if they didn't have the science to understand it yet—but all have increased in scope and impact as we've become more intelligent creatures. We've become less fixated and dependent on the concrete world and more focused on our inner-selves, but also on imaginary overlays of the physical world: societies, social networks, relationships.

Go back a few generations and you'll find many people worked sixteen-hour days on the farm, every day, no breaks, no time to do anything else, except for birthing the occasional baby. Under such conditions, it's no surprise that it was common to set aside unsubstantial concerns, like feeling intellectually unchallenged or philosophically unfulfilled. One needed to exert all of one's time and energy on survival.

Liberating ourselves from that burden has left us with more time and energy to spend on internal exploration, which in turn has changed our perception of how important these psychological struggles really are. That we're able to be attentive to things like fulfillment and happiness, and doing work we can be proud of, and not feeling depressed, is a good sign no matter how debilitating these problems can be for those who suffer from them. That their suffering is now considered an issue, and one we can spend time addressing, is an indication of progress.

But even these issues are fueled by, and will likely be solved as a consequence of, language. We're now capable of describing our existential ennui, our lack of motivation in the morning, and the triggering of a fight-or-flight response when a car backfires with remarkable accuracy. Being capable of calling out and communicating these issues, internally, but also to others within our communities, allows us to identify, assess, and sometimes solve these problems. In the past, these concerns would have remained undescribed and unlabeled, and as such, unaddressable.

Language, at the most basic level and at the most complex, is an invention that has allowed us to organize and share knowledge. It allows us to discuss the environment and discuss ourselves. It allows us to identify problems and come up with solutions to them.

Though language has helped us evolve in many positive ways, we've also seen a number of malevolent mutations that threaten the foundations upon which society is built.

Both a convergence and a splintering of language are occurring right now; the pace is rapid, and the scale is immense.

The former is the result of globalization: cultures creating lines of communication with other cultures, then actively engaging and trading with each other every day. These predictable points of contact cause a spillover of cultural ideology, and so Japan's social mores, pop stars, and ideologies have become popular in even geographically distant, otherwise-unconnected places like Estonia.

As this occurs, we also see an exchange of casual and practical language. It can take time for this to happen—look at the United States and its slow-growth relationship with the Spanish language, for instance—but the rate at which we receive and parse data of this kind is increasing because we're no longer limited to chatting and trading with the national neighbor next door. The whole world is open for business and there are advantages in clear communication.

The development and availability of intuitive translation tools have amplified this effect. Such software makes in-depth knowledge of another culture's language less necessary to instigate a connection, which allows us to make more rapid, tenuous connections. Over time, these transitory relationships have the potential to turn into something larger, and to make our understanding of the other culture more thorough. Google Translate will help you understand that your friend from Thailand is telling you about his new cat, but it won't make the connection that "five" translates to "ha," and so when he types "555," he's saying "ha ha ha." A more complex understanding of other cultures often emerges as a consequence of these tools, but not from the tools themselves.

The cross-pollination of language is not just a sharing of words, it's a sharing of habits and priorities. Such exchanges occur between members of the same societies who are part of different demographic cultures, as well. A recent example of this is the emergence of emoji as a secondary language used within text-based messages. Emoji is an iconographic language that began its life as emoticons—faces and other expressive symbols made out of semi-colons, question marks, and other alphanumeric figures—on Japanese phones in the 1990s. Phones began supporting graphical versions of these icons that same decade, and Apple's iPhone operating system brought emoji to the US, allowing American users to send smileys instead of words with one tap of their finger. The Android operating system started doing the same not long after that, and today, people of all age demographics and cultures are using icon sets of this kind in their communications.

What's notable is that this language system migrated first from Japan, then to mostly coastal, mostly creative-industry types in the US, and then to their youthful brethren throughout the country. The widespread popularity of later model emoji-enabled iPhones meant that this capability was available to people from a greater diversity of economic and age demographics. The explosion of the Android ecosystem on low-cost devices around the world meant that people from Kolkata to Reykjavík were suddenly able to send the same smiling poop icon to each other.

Emoji is a success story of language, in that it provides us with a shared method of communication, a shared unit of labelling and understanding. If I'm texting someone with whom I don't share a single word, I can still communicate simple ideas via these images, and they to me. That's remarkable and valuable.

The downside of this is what happens in the time in between initial adoption by trendsetters and the eventual adoption by everyone. It's during that gap in time, which can span a few months or a few decades depending on the innovation that's being disseminated, that some portion of the population is able to more easily communicate with one another, while others are left out of that conversation.

In the case of emoji, this left-out group contained the over-thirty age demographic, a group of people who began to feel old any time they'd check to see what the kids were up to. Yes, it might have been obvious that these teenagers and twenty-somethings were using cute little graphics to chat with each other, but for many of us in those early days, pre-emoji-adoption, it all just seemed so ridiculous. Why not type words at each other, rather than a meaningless stream of hands-in-the-air and dancing girl icons? And why not use correct punctuation while you're at it?

During the latter part of the early days of this trend, emoji keyboards were available to everyone. The barrier wasn't technological, it was cultural. And that cultural barrier meant that, although we were talking about the same things, because we were using different languages to discuss them, we ended up talking right past each other. Entire cycles of information, cultural norms, and internet memes flew right by those of us who didn't adopt emoji until later. We sort of understood what was happening, but we didn't truly get it.

This is not just an emoji-based issue. If you want to see a stark example of people discussing the same things but talking past each other, look no further than partisan political news.

When we discuss abortion and women's rights in the United States, the opposite and oppositional Pro-Life and Pro-Choice movements dominate the conversation. Both of these groups' names are examples of what's called "political framing," which means they're attempting to present their side in the best possible light, while simultaneously hoping to show the flaws in the opposing camp's stance.

"Pro-Choice" is a label that says we want to respect an individual's liberty to decide for themselves. A woman should have control over what happens to her own body, and anyone who argues otherwise is attempting to stifle freedom.

"Pro-Life" is a label that says we want to preserve the life of an unborn child at all costs, and anyone who would act otherwise is pro-death, or anti-baby.

Terms like "unborn child," commonly used by Pro-Lifers, are also examples of political framing. Referring to a bundle of stem cells and tissue as an unborn child is a way of shaping the public's opinion about abortion. It's a use of language that, while not scientifically accurate, is often successful at winning a debate before either side has even presented their arguments.

Both sides in this particular issue, and all sides in almost any issue, make use of this type of idea framing. The result is that conservative talking heads use one vocabulary when talking about the issue of abortion, while liberal talking heads use a completely different vocabulary when talking about the same. You could listen to the most extreme examples from both sides and it would seem perfectly clear, by the way they frame the issues, that anyone who disagrees with them is not just wrong, but also a morally bankrupt individual.

The level of sophistication in how we frame discussions has evolved from sticks and stones to AK-47s. We've become so skilled at shaping discussions through the language we use, and the public has become so accustomed to hearing their side's chosen vocabulary, that it's possible to determine an unfamiliar radio show's bias after listening to ten seconds of audio. Even absent an argument or any greater context, listeners understand, reflexively, that these are not "their people" speaking to them. They change channels or tune out.

Many of the larger, more mainstream news sources still do their best to keep things neutral—the *Associated Press*, for instance, uses the terms "abortion rights" and "anti-abortion" in lieu of "Pro-Choice" and "Pro-Life"—but many networks have done away with the veil of balance completely. *Fox News* and *MSNBC* have staked out opposite claims on the political spectrum, for instance, often blending editorial with news, with predictable results. It's possible to watch the same supposedly unbiased news story presented on these two news networks and come away with two very different ideas of what actually happened. It's remarkable that we can present the same facts in such different ways, using such different frames. It's no wonder we so reliably speak past one another when it comes to certain issues.

This is not a new trend. There have been partisan newspapers and periodicals for as long as there has been a printing press. But our capacity to communicate as we do today, as quickly and as integrally as we do, has amplified the impact of these divisions.

The algorithms in our social networks and search engines ostensibly exist to help us find the most relevant results when we're looking for something, but relevancy is relative. These algorithms need to earn money for their master, and that means showing us things that incentivize clicks and interaction. These platforms earn money through advertising, and that means they earn money when we stick around and click things, and when we share content that other people interact with and click. Keeping us online and engaged throughout the day is a survival requisite for these companies, so it should be no surprise that "relevant" to them has a different meaning than for us.

Google and Facebook have both invested in technological infrastructure that helps more people around the world connect to the internet. This is a noble effort in some ways, but it's also an effort that helps boost their bottom lines. More people online means more people clicking and interacting and sharing, which in turn means more ad dollars.

It should be no surprise, then, that these algorithms show us things that will be most likely to evoke emotional response in their users. What's more likely to get you to like, share, or to leave a comment: a well-balanced long-read about something educational, or a timely news item with an outrageous headline designed to make you feel anger, sadness, hope, excitement, pity, love, or depression?

These platforms have reinforced our "filter bubbles." That is, spaces in which we only see things that are relevant to us, and which make us feel the most feels. The modern iterations of such spaces are shaped by software that know a whole lot about our habits, preferences, and relationships. Inside these filter bubbles, we're presented with information that reinforces our existing beliefs using the vocabulary we've been trained to expect from people who agree with us. We're typically only presented with opposing perspectives when they are outrage-inducing or ridiculous.

This is not a novel creation of the Information Age. We've built our own societally reinforced filter bubbles for generations, surrounding ourselves with people and ideas that reinforce our existing biases, while ignoring information and people who would poke holes in our beliefs. But our new tools, our wondrous technology, has amplified the effectiveness of these bubbles, and made them harder to pop, or even see. The consequences of this are many.

First, we seldom experience cognitive dissonance, which is the feeling of discomfort associated with being exposed to information that contradicts our existing beliefs. This dissonance is a vital component of changing our minds and adjusting our views, and without it, without feeling that we might be wrong about something and therefore it's probably important to check our math and learn more about the subject we've been armchair-philosophizing about on Facebook, we stand little chance of ever tempering our extreme, unjustifiable views. In fact, we're even more likely to indulge in more extreme versions of our existing beliefs because our every opinion seems to be reaffirmed by the information we're given, our every question and quibble laid to rest by the data we're fed.

Second, it means we're increasingly likely to view anyone who disagrees with us as dangerous idiots who can't see the obvious truth, rather than people who simply disagree with us. The opposition no longer holds legitimate ideas that we disagree with but understand, but instead are spreading inane, obvious falsehoods. They're dangerous, we think, not merely wrong. And all the news we receive from within our bubbles seems to reaffirm this perspective.

Third, it tethers us to a few sources of information that reinforce our chosen ideologies. If we agree with the editorial slant of one news site over another, we begin to see more news from that site over time. Eventually, we see little that isn't from that particular organization, or others just like it, and our ability to investigate and disprove what we're told becomes severely atrophied.

Finally, these filter bubbles make us less aware that there's even disagreement with our chosen view of events. If my bubble serves up the content that's most likely to keep me around, it's not incentivized to show me things that might make me feel uncomfortable. It's completely possible, then, that I might live my life completely unaware that contradictory information even exists. My opinion is presented to me whole, which means there's no need for me to cobble together my own. This makes it easier for algorithms to predict what I'll want to see, but a lot more difficult for anyone who wants to form their own opinions, using many sources.

There's a great deal of power in being able to shape a person's view of not just an individual news item, but also the world and the people in it. If you decide who are the friends and who are the enemies, who are the heroes and who are the villains, what are the facts and what are the lies, then you control not just a person's opinions and the words they use to discuss them, but also how they vote, who they interact with, and what sorts of military conflicts they'll support.

The situation we find ourselves in today isn't the consequence of a grand conspiracy, but rather the impact of language, how we use it, and how it's evolving. It's the result of many groups seeing an advantage in using language to keep us on edge and worried, or inspired and fighting a particular fight. A democratic system of governance requires an educated electorate to operate, and the misuse and weaponization of language hinders us in that regard. It keeps us engaged, but ignorant.

The coming years will be in part defined by whether we're able to re-learn how to talk to each other, and how we might do so in productive ways. It's fun to win an argument, or to embarrass someone you consider to be the opposition, but is that productive? Does it incentivize them to pay attention to you and what you're saying? Or does it just reinforce existing opinions and ideologies? Are you rallying the troops, or are you actually reaching someone new with your words? Are you incentivizing them to pay attention and parse what you're saying?

How might you communicate across demographics? How might you reach younger people, older people, people who have different economic circumstances from you, and people who communicate via voice, text, or video, while you prefer some other medium?

Perhaps most importantly, what are you saying to begin

with? And is what you're saying worth sharing?

Our communication tools motivate us to talk and tweet and Instagram and share videos all the time, because those are the activities that prop up their bottom line. But saturating these channels just for the sake of not having to deal with silence, of having to think our own thoughts and listen to our own internal monologue for a while, is part of the problem.

The tools we have available today allow us to connect with one another and to express ourselves in remarkable ways, but they're only valuable if we use them intentionally. If we stop using them reflexively and compulsively, and instead think about what we're using them for, how we're using them, and how we might better exploit the powers they give us.

Language is only valuable if we say something, and communication is only valuable if it's transmitting something of worth.

Freedom & Security

There's a quote attributed to Benjamin Franklin that goes something like this: "Those who would give up their freedom in exchange for security deserve neither."

His words were originally intended to show his support for new taxes that were to be collected by the US Government to aid the military against the French and Native Americans, with which the burgeoning US National Guard had been clashing. The true quote goes like this: "Those who would give up essential Liberty, to purchase a little temporary Safety, deserve neither Liberty nor Safety."

"Contextomy" is the practice of intentionally taking someone's words out of context for a particular gain. In this case, Franklin's words were over time iteratively revised and taken out of the context of their original letter so they could be used in support of causes as varied as warning the public about communications security apparatus violations, to full-throated support of a capitalistic free market.

Regardless of whether Franklin himself was the original coiner of the rearranged quote, it's still a compellingly phrased idea, and one that's worth exploring.

Freedom and security are two things that many modern

cultures value, or claim to value, but which often seem to be at odds with each other, because the ostensible requirements to keep both freedom and security intact can seem zero-sum. If we elevate our level of freedom, we open ourselves up to abuse or attack. If we increase our level of security, we necessarily give up some measure of freedom in the trade-off.

What makes this discussion, and many discussions, all the more difficult to have is that opposing sides are often using different definitions of the words in question, and resultantly we might think we're talking about the same thing, when in fact we're merely speaking past each other.

"Freedom" is a word that might mean something different to every person who uses it. Does being free mean that you can wear whatever clothing you want? Does it mean you can work wherever you can get a job, and marry whomever you want? Does it mean that you should be free to have a job, even if you're not providing any particular value for the person paying you? Does it mean freedom of movement within and across borders? Perhaps it's the freedom of electing officials to represent you and your priorities? The freedom to feel represented even if your candidate didn't get elected? Is it the freedom to worship however you choose? Does freedom mean police won't harass you? Does freedom mean you don't have to feel encircled by people who act and look different from you? Does your freedom allow you to say whatever you like to anyone, even if your words are meant to inflict harm? Are you free to restrict other people's freedoms? If a stranger gets married to someone who you don't believe they should be able to marry, does that infringe on your freedom to live in accordance with your convictions? Are you free to wear whatever you like, even if your headscarf seems menacing to some people, or your baggy clothing seems like a security threat to police?

Are your freedoms dependent on other people having fewer freedoms? And if so, whose freedoms do we prioritize?

If you zoom out a bit you'll find that the only reason we have freedom, using whatever definition you might choose for the word, is because we have a security apparatus in place that defends it from forces which might restrict our freedoms for their own. On a large scale, that means conquest by a ruling class that might have less reason to provide us with the freedoms our current elected leadership allows us. On a smaller scale, that could mean regional and even individual defense against criminals who might wish us physical harm, or who might want to take our stuff.

It's common to think that we might be freer without any such security in place, but in most societies, those that exist today and in the past, this probably wouldn't be the case.

Our civilization is structured on the assumption of scarcity, and everything from economics to how we interact with each other reflects this. If we ever develop technologies or systems that allow us to become a post-scarcity civilization—that is, we all have plenty of what we need to survive and thrive, and therefore nothing to gain from taking from others—then this could change. There's less incentive to steal something from your neighbor when you already have or can get that same thing without resorting to criminality. And there's less reason to defend against such theft if you know you can easily get another of whatever was taken without hassle.

But in the here and now, not a single post-scarcity society exists on Earth, and that means we're forced to find a balance that allows us to enjoy as many freedoms as possible while still feeling protected by the societal armor of a well-honed military, police force, and intelligence infrastructure.

Autocratic regimes, those ruled by one person or group without democratic fail-safes, often provide their people with watered-down or faux freedoms. Some go to great lengths to perform fake elections with results that are pre-determined, and sometimes they'll even use the language of liberal democracy while rigging the system and arresting or killing dissenters when the cameras are turned off. Alterations to the permanent record and to the news can cause people to question their own memories. Autocrats do this, in part, because restricting the rights of everyone within a country should, in theory, ensure more predictability and lessen the chances of violent uprisings or coups against the government.

This isn't always how it works in practice, but the theory is sound. If you can convince your people that they are safer when there are fewer outsiders among them, and that the freedoms they sacrifice are the price they pay for safety, then you're pretty well set.

There are stable autocratic regimes in existence all around the world, and though the 20th century was a democratic political story for the most part, and though there are immense economic and diplomatic benefits for those countries that have moved toward a Greek-derived, Iroquois-amplified, Western philosophical ideal of openness, republicanism, pluralism, and intersectionality, there are still cultures that seem to be historically primed, or perhaps just currently ripe, for strongman leadership. There are also cultures that have tried democracy on for size and found it to be a chafing, awkward fit.

It should be said that there is nothing inherently superior about democracy, or any other method of governance. It is not the One True Governing System, nor is it likely to be the last we'll ever dominantly adopt around the world. Governments as institutions, in their current form, could one day become passé, at which point the idea of democracy would seem just as backwards to future people as feudalistic systems, with their royalty and castles and serfs, seem to most of us today.

But there are reasons democratic systems really caught on in the mid-19th century. The benefits of such systems, especially in a rapidly globalizing, increasingly interconnected world, are many.

Statistically, democracies are a lot less likely to go to war with each other. That's a huge security benefit. And again without security, none of this democracy stuff would work. Without defenses, someone else would swoop in and suck up all the resources and probably swaddle the defenseless, freedom-loving people in so many rules and restrictions they'd come to wonder if that moment of liberty they seem to remember was real or just a pleasant dream.

On a smaller scale, security means putting thieves in jail so we don't feel like we have to defend our property continuously or risk losing it to armed gangs. It means giving out expensive traffic tickets to dissuade people from driving through red lights so that it's less likely we'll be plowed into by careless drivers while commuting, or while taking the kids out to dinner. It means having checkpoints at airports and at national monuments to search cars and check individuals for weapons, which is intended to reduce the chances of someone blowing themselves up, along with innocent bystanders, to make an ideological point.

I very seldom walk down the street in a US city and worry that I'm going to be attacked, robbed, or threatened in any way. This is not something I can say about all the cities I've visited around the world. But being a straight, middle class white guy, my experience with police officers is no doubt wildly different from that of a young black man, an older Latino woman, a brown-skinned Muslim of any age or gender, or a gay teenager in the South. I've heard stories, and I've seen first-hand the consequences of the intimidation and even relatively minor abuses of power that take place between police and citizens. I believe in most cases that these abuses aren't the result of horrible people taking up the badge, but rather a systemic issue with how we enforce not just laws, but perceived norms. We don't just give out tickets because someone was driving too fast, we give out tickets because we believe these individuals are the type of people who do this regularly, and who were distracted because they live their lives in a certain way and therefore deserve to get a ticket because they're bad. This same bias influences who gets frisked for weapons, who gets guns pointed at them for minor infractions, and who gets put in jail for possessing small amounts of illicit substances.

Studies have shown that from a very young age we feel an innate desire to enforce norms on each other. Little kids do it, sometimes to rabid extremes, punishing anyone who doesn't fall into line with what seems to be the schoolyard consensus. They even call out their parents when they feel Mom or Dad hasn't lived up to cultural expectations or has broken a rule they perceive to be unbreakable.

It's worth remembering that we cannot know what's going on in another person's head. We're far more likely to see a stranger's actions through our own lens than to attempt to look through theirs. When a stranger does something we perceive to be wrong, we're likely to imbue that action with malice, whereas they might only see a harmless act. Our biases and prejudices color our perception of the world, and recognizing this, and working it into our math when we're attempting to discern what's happening, is one of the better ways to avoid ascribing guilt or menace to situations that are honest mistakes or blatant misinterpretations.

Viewing the world through just one lens warps what we see. Being aware of that distortion gives us the opportunity to correct for it.

If we're going to fully benefit from our security apparatus, we'll need to separate our biases from the strict rules we put into place. Our rules shouldn't target individuals or specific groups, and should allow us to enforce regulations that prevent victimization, rather than accidentally create new victims.

Mid-2016, a series of regulations were passed in France which banned beach-goers from wearing burkinis, swimwear made for Muslim women who wish to cover themselves but still visit the beach comfortably, at many beaches and resorts in the country. These regulations were passed in response to a sequence of deadly terrorist attacks perpetrated by Muslim radicals in the area.

The rationale of these regulations was to ensure that people who wanted to visit the beach would feel safe, rather than wondering if they'd become a victim in the next attack. This is a legitimate goal: our security apparatus should allow us feel secure enough to go about our day without worrying that we'll be injured, killed, or otherwise victimized.

The tactic used in this case, however, sacrificed the needs and freedoms of a large group of people as a trade-off. Muslim women, who for both personal and religious reasons do not want to show their skin in public, would now be forced to either expose that which they do not want to expose, or avoid the beaches and resorts completely. In an effort to protect one group, another was victimized, and this victimization was made explicit when a Muslim woman lounging on the beach had her burkini torn from her body by a French police officer. Many other burkini wearers weren't attacked by police for defying the regulation, but were instead fined for wearing the wrong clothing in the wrong place.

There are several different ways to view these regulations and how they were enforced. All of these views are potentially right, depending on the lens through which you view the world, how you define freedom, and perhaps how you view these specific events and the people involved in a larger context.

One perspective is that laws exist to protect the majority of people the majority of the time; a Utilitarian stance. If a particular religion and its vestments are increasingly associated with violence, shouldn't we do our best to dissuade people from flaunting associations with that religion? No one has yet, as far as I'm aware, hidden a bomb in a burkini in France, but if the burkini itself has become a symbol to the majority of people, much like the swastika in Germany or Klansman hood in the US, shouldn't we regulate such things? Should we allow someone in full Ku Klux Klansman garb to waltz into an African American church and intimidate everyone there without pushback?

Some would say yes, we should. The free speech-centric perspective on this situation would be that people can say whatever they want, wear whatever they want, and even, with few exceptions, do whatever they want. So long as these words, clothes, and actions aren't physically hurting anyone else, why should we ban them? Yes, some people will be insulted. Yes, some people will be intimidated. But the law exists to keep people from physically hurting other people, and if we start restricting things because they may offend or psychologically harm someone, then we'll soon be left with nothing we can safely say, do, or wear. The nature of a democracy is that we can disagree with one another, and our country should be a safe space in the sense that we can all believe whatever we like, and express ourselves however we like provided we don't impede anyone else's right to do the same. The concept of "safe spaces" on campuses and hate crimes as a separate consideration from normal crimes are contrary to this idea, but so is the limiting of what one can wear or say or do, up to the point that such expression becomes something else entirely. In other words, you have many rights, but the right to not be offended is not one of them.

Another perspective, and a common one, I think, is that it's complicated.

Many of us fall somewhere between extremes on this issue because we can see that, yes, it's vital that we have free speech, and yes, it makes sense that it must be unfettered free speech or the whole things becomes meaningless. If someone I disagree with can't express themselves today, perhaps I won't be able to express myself tomorrow, because my opinions have become the unpopular ones?

That said, maybe just this one group should be restricted, or maybe just this one case of bullying on the internet should be clamped down on, or maybe we should ban just this one type of clothing worn by people who have become associated with violent acts?

The rallying cry for this standpoint might be something like, "Yes, free speech all the time for everyone! But not that one person who's doing that clearly horrible thing."

Unfortunately, "horrible" is another incredibly subjective term. Ask one hundred people for a definition and example, and you'll get one hundred different answers. The opinion that these things are complicated, then, is itself riddled with complexity, because it means the things on which we willingly bend are more likely to victimize some groups over others.

It may be that we want complete and absolute free speech, except for people who are Muslims. But it could also be that we want complete and absolute free speech, except for people who say racist things, or spread conspiracy theories, or question the rights of the LGBT community to marry whomever they like. When we see this particular option as appealing, we're seeing it through the lens of our own biases. It's a seemingly easy, potent solution because the legitimacy of our beliefs is obvious. Who wouldn't want to silence the racists? But from another person's standpoint, it's also obvious that we should absolutely keep people of different races from marrying or reproducing, and that racists should be the only ones able to freely speak.

I think authoritarianism taps into a desire the majority of us have lurking just beneath the surface. It's not something we like to admit because the atrocities and casual violence that occur under many authoritarian regimes are not things with which we want to be associated. But given the option, I'm guessing there are very few people who wouldn't put an authoritarian into power under the right circumstances.

If given the power, who wouldn't want to see the most ideal, optimal version of their beliefs made manifest? If given the power to, say, make sure that only well-informed people can vote, or to make sure that homophobic violence will be brutally punished, or to put all the bankers involved in financial scandals behind bars for life, rather than protecting them and bailing them out?

It's a heady feeling, thinking about what you could accomplish if given the power to do so. If able to sweep away all the dissenting voices. But doing so, leveraging that power, that ability to act unilaterally, would be an authoritarian act. The premise of democracy is that there is a push-pull between different people with different points of view, and we are ostensibly stronger because of this diversity of ideas and priorities.

Even with the very best of intentions, if you were to enforce your will on a country full of people, you would become someone's Mussolini, someone's Hitler, someone's Nero. You'd be a tyrant to those who don't have the same values as you, and though most of us live in filter bubbles that reinforce our values and reflect our ideas back at us, making us feel that our ideas are the dominant ones, or even the only ones that matter, this is absolutely not the case.

If you believe wholeheartedly that enforcing your ideals on the world would be the best possible thing for everyone, that's fine. You're allowed to feel that way. But that means you cannot claim that democracy, liberty, pluralism, or any of the other principles we tend to hold up as important in the free world today are key to your value system. You cannot both value open discourse and autonomously decide to change everything for everyone because you and only you know best.

This is worth remembering when engaged in a disagreement, whether on the societal or interpersonal level. If we can have meaningful discussions, change minds through rational argument, and instigate change—not through the barrel of a gun but through the power of our ideas—we're living up to a set of standards that have typically resulted in positive things. There have been growing pains and missteps, but the general trajectory of human well-being since the development and widespread adoption of democratic systems has been undeniably upward. It's tempting to think about how much better the world would be if we could just take our intellectual opponents out of the equation, but history indicates otherwise.

Moral malleability tends to be a positive thing. It's important to be able to change one's mind when new information becomes available, and to change one's actions accordingly.

This asset, however, becomes a liability when it's shaky in the face of real, concrete issues. An "it's complicated" model of thinking allows us to avoid cognitive dissonance—that feeling of discomfort we get when the real world hits us with information that seems to conflict with our existing biases and understanding—but it also means we're likely to be wobbly on issues of real significance and vital importance. It's easy, bordering on lazy, to say, "People should be able to wear whatever they like," but to then weaken your stance when government officials say otherwise. "Okay, you can wear whatever you like, but not that one thing, because it makes some people uncomfortable."

If your actual position, your truly moral stance, is that freedom requires we make sacrifices, and among those sacrifices is not wearing burkinis on the beach and not wearing ski masks in banks, because both decrease the perceived security of public spaces, that's fine. That's a consistent stance, and although there are still troubling issues about how a burkini is in any way actually dangerous, rather than it just being a race/religion-based restriction, this is at least a consistent judgment rather than a fracture in our ideology that we've allowed to slip in under the radar. When ideological cracks go unaddressed, not only do we find ourselves with opinions we'll defend to the death but cannot justify, we also fail to acknowledge that we hold internally conflicting views, and as such probably can't trust much of what we believe. And that leaves us susceptible to dominance by demagogues and authoritarians who will gladly tell us what to think.

What we do with a better understanding of our own values and beliefs is for each of us to decide for ourselves. We might keep these ideas to ourselves, or we might act upon them to shape the larger collective, to ensure that something less ideal doesn't infringe upon our ability to live as we prefer.

In societies that enjoy some semblance of freedom, there are many paths we can take, from protesting and contributing monetarily to relevant causes, to getting personally involved in politics to ensure that morally sound policies are enacted.

Options are limited in more restrictive societies, but there are always ways to warp or crack the infrastructure in which you live. It's just a matter of finding weaknesses, flaws in the structure, and making them known. Widespread knowledge of structural flaws can lead to fixes in those systems without needing to bring the whole thing crumbling down. Sometimes a wholesale rebuild will be necessary, but often it's safer and faster to incite iteration rather than revolution.

We have the power to change things, in big ways and small, if we choose to accept responsibility for that power and act in ways we find to be morally justifiable. Recognizing the conflicts and relationships between things like freedom and security, and within our own internal systems of morality, is vital to understanding what we might do, but also why and how.

We aren't required to do anything at all with this knowledge, but it's nice to know we can if we like. And that if we do work toward change, our goals will be aligned with our actual beliefs, rather than convenient mistruths or ideas we've been fed by others.

Experimentation

Science is as often misunderstood as it is debated. This is in part a consequence of having been told since birth that our opinions are just as good as anyone else's.

This is true, of course, in the sense that you are absolutely allowed to believe that the color green is better than blue, or that hip-hop music is better than a waltz. These are completely subjective opinions, and you and whomever you're disagreeing with can both be right while holding completely different opinions because you're expressing the results of a purely internal deliberation. No one knows your flavor preferences better than you, no one knows what kind of music makes you want to dance better than you.

It is not true, however, that our opinions are "just as good" when it comes to anything else. If you believe climate experts should take your amateur opinion that climate change is not real seriously, you're mistaken. You are completely welcome to believe that climate change is a hoax perpetrated by the Chinese, and that the whole of the scientific world, except for a few scientists who are on the payroll of the fossil fuel industries, are involved in a major conspiracy to make us believe it's real. But the rest of the world has little reason to take you seriously. Regardless of the celebrity of a person who might hold such opinions, the opinion itself is not equal to one that's supported by evidence and the credibility of professionals who say otherwise. Strong belief is not the same as evidence based on knowledge and backed by expertise.

Our understanding of the world, the galaxy, the universe in which we live, is increased through a scientific model, which allows us to posit ideas and then test them systematically. This method has proven to be immensely useful and accurate, especially when paired with things like rationality and empiricism, which help us figure out what happened and what might happen next.

Through science, we observe the world around us, then attempt to explain and understand it. Instead of saying, "That feathery creature just flew over my head: it is probably lighter than air," and then leaving it at that, through science we're able to make that observation, test it under controlled conditions, recognize that birds are not, in fact, lighter than air, and then run an array of new tests to see what might actually explain how these little beasts can fly. This process involves culling variables that might impact our results, changing a single variable, which allows us to see the impact of that single change on the overall experiment, and running parallel "control" experiments without those changes, to ensure our results are not explainable by random variation.

This is a radically simplified explanation of how science is conducted, but even when fully fleshed out, it's a relatively simple concept. We observe, we experiment, we refine and experiment some more, and we eventually learn something that we can express and act upon.

Being able to explain what we learn through this process is vital, as that's what allows us to more fully understand reality. It also allows us to sometimes make use of what we discover, harnessing it for use in our technology, our tools.

The development of the lithium ion battery, which is found in almost every portable device today, from smartphones to hearing aids, was predicated on the results of scientific research. Gobs of experiments had to be conducted to understand how lithium might hold a charge, then how to make it hold more, and then how to release its energy little by little, the right amount over the right period of time. Then we had to figure out how to optimize it for rechargeability within a device, using existing charging standards. Many of the resources poured into new inventions are expended on the initial research and development stage. Not the production, but the scientific process of trial and error and document and adjust, and eventually, some understanding of what we're dealing with and how this new knowledge might be used.

What we end up with at the end of the process is the ability to say, "This is real. This is a thing and here's how it works."

Of course, anyone, at any time, can say that about anything. The reason a scientifically backed statement holds more weight is that, because of the tests and iterations involved, we are as certain as we can be that not only does it work this way, but we know why. We can understand and explain the underlying mechanics. We can say, "If I do this, this will happen," and it does.

We can't just say, "Climate change is real." In the scientific community, such a statement requires evidence. It needs to be strongly supported by data, experimentation, and vast amounts of research.

Anything within science is prone to change. One of the most misunderstood aspects of science is that it seems like everything is just a theory. This is true, in a sense, because science is set up in such a way that it adjusts and rewires based on new information. If the scientific community believes, based on sufficient quantities of experimentation and collected data, that dinosaurs had scales and were brownish-green, but then later finds more complete fossils with feathers and new research results that indicate they were probably brightly colored and wore light to heavy plumage, dino-loving scientists will pivot on a dime. Their previous evidence was incomplete, and now, as it's become more complete, their conclusions about what that information indicates must also change. Far from being arrogant intellectuals, scientists have an intense, ingrained sense of humility that allows them to change their well-defined worldview when warranted.

They do not cleave to their existing beliefs because it's uncomfortable to change. They respect evidence. Rather than trying to make new evidence fit within their worldview, they will remake their worldview to fit the evidence.

This is one difference between a scientifically held belief—one backed by fact and observation and empiricism and a model that refines and culls outdated ideas—and beliefs held out of tradition, emotion, or dogma.

You may believe the sun was created when two super beings the size of the Milky Way had sex. You may believe the Earth is perched atop the shell of the Galactic Tortoise. You may believe the space gods that control life on Earth are invisible and therefore we don't see them as they manipulate happenings on our planet. But there's no way to disprove or prove these assertions, so these ideas, these beliefs, have no more or less credibility than any other claim that cannot be proven or disproven. You have every right to believe these things, but that doesn't mean they hold their own against conclusions that are testable and verifiable.

We can use this method, this experimental process, to iterate not just scientifically and technologically as a society, but also personally and interpersonally as individuals.

Many of us fall into rhythms relatively early in life, and then decide, either consciously or subconsciously, that the rhythm we've come to know is the totality of life. This is it.

This is how things are. The evidence of me experiencing life in this fashion seems to support the hypothesis that this is how life is meant to be; the only way it can be.

But this isn't the case.

Sometimes an outside force gusts into our lives and changes everything. It rearranges the furniture and pushes us from one job into another. Maybe it causes us to break up with our significant other and meet someone new.

But most often we have to be those winds of change. We are the only forces capable of regularly and intentionally changing our lives, hopefully for the better, and that means either acquiring a taste for randomness and unpredictability, allowing outside forces to determine our direction, or taking on the responsibilities of a citizen scientist and experimenting with our lives as if they're lithium ion batteries or flying beasts.

What I've found works well for me in this regard is making sure I have two or three experiments going at a time, each applying to different elements of my life.

I recently decided to set aside a portion of each morning, during which time I stick to a well-defined schedule. I wake up, do a quick workout, sit quietly and think for ten minutes, check my email and the news for fifteen minutes, write for two hours, and then get on with my day.

This routine isn't particularly taxing. I was already writing two hours or more a day, and I have a more regular and intense workout routine that I perform each night. But in formalizing this habit, I wanted to see what it would feel like to front-load those activities to the morning, rather than having them fall wherever they may, scattered to land at unpredictable points throughout my day. I wanted to see if there would be any benefit to that added structure before I segue back into my far less regulated lifestyle.

I've decided to run this experiment for a month, at which

point I'll stop and assess. I'll determine what I learned from it, if the habit is beneficial in some way, and ask myself how I might adjust it further to amplify those benefits. I may also decide to do away with it completely, either because it has proved to be more hassle than benefit, or because it seems some other habit may prove more beneficial.

This flavor of lifestyle experimentation is a far cry from anything that would be allowed in a lab. It's absolutely not science. But introducing experimentation into our lives can be valuable, so long as we're willing to make observations, adjust variables, keep track of what we learn as a result of those tweaks, and then either make long-lasting changes or flip back to where we started, having learned something that can inform our next round of experiments.

Lifestyle experimentation is a means of instigating changes in your own life. It allows you to take a few steps away from familiarity and comfort, secure in the knowledge that you still know the way back, rather than hurling yourself into the unknown, perhaps losing the best of what you had before. This approach can trigger personal iteration: a series of small, consistent improvements. It also vastly increases the odds you'll discover something huge and meaningful and important about your habits, your lifestyle, or yourself.

The adjustment I've made to my mornings may prove to be nothing. It will maybe become a lovely addition to my day. It may also be the source of immensely positive, life-changing consequences.

This morning habit could prove to be a net-negative. It could be something I'm happy to see go after the experimental period to which I've committed. Perhaps it makes me less productive, less happy, and less likely to achieve what I want to achieve.

I have no way of knowing which it will be until I give it a try. But by keeping track of the consequences of this habit, how I'm feeling, and the work I'm creating for the month, I'll know which is which by the time it's over. This is useful for me as an individual, but it's also a concept that works well on scale.

In some cities around the world, today, a small selection of people are given a guaranteed basic income each month by their governments.

This income isn't large—it ranges between $800 and $2,000 per month—but it's sufficient to pay their rent, shop for groceries, and get health care, in most cases. The goal is to see what happens when people are provided with enough money to pay for the bare essentials, as governments are trying to decide how best to ameliorate the negative consequences of rapid technological development.

Many people have already been left without work as their jobs have been automated. This is happening around the world, and seems likely to be a continuing, booming trend. Entire industries are disappearing in the blink of an eye, leaving the human employees, those whose skills align with that particular type of work, out in the cold.

The introduction of automation into these industries can be a positive thing, but only if these workers aren't left homeless and hungry as a result. Providing a guaranteed basic income could allow them to stay housed and fed while they retrain for new jobs, or perhaps as they take some time between careers to be with their families, indulge in hobbies, create art, or whatever else might strike their fancy.

This method of bulwarking against the downsides of industrial progress may not work. It may be that if people know they have enough money coming in each month to survive without working, then no one will work. It may be that inflation will render a person's monthly guaranteed income meaningless, and the people who receive it will be left without the bare minimum sustenance it's meant to provide. It may be that the system itself proves unsustainable, and the cost of providing and distributing these funds outweighs the benefits of doing so.

But it may be that implementing such a system changes everything for the better. It may be the most direct, best way to alleviate both poverty and concerns about technology taking our jobs. It may stimulate a wave of innovation and creativity, liberating the populace from the shackles of tedious work, leading to even more implementation of automation, which in turn frees the human mind to pursue the things it's best at and which it finds challenging and fulfilling, rather than spending all its bandwidth bagging groceries and collecting trash.

Again, we'll never know until we try. And the best way to try something like this is to experiment, over time, tweaking many different variables.

We have the capacity, the capability, the will, and the drive to instigate positive change. On the personal, societal, and humanity-wide scale, we can be observers, imaginers, and experimenters. This, over time, should help us become better versions of ourselves.

Filters & Boundaries

We've never been more capable, we humans.

We've done a remarkable job of adjusting our environment to suit our needs. If the elements are threatening or uncomfortable, we build shelters. If the temperature isn't to our liking, we build devices that warm or cool the air inside those shelters. If the land doesn't naturally provide enough food for the population we desire we rearrange it, we breed it, we genetically modify it to ensure it provides us with the right calories, the right nutrition, and enough energy to build more structures, to warm more chilly air, to plow more fields.

There are some who see this tendency of ours as a negative habit, and at the extremes, it certainly can be. When we overdo it, we not only demolish the environment, we also harm ourselves. We poison the soil and toxify the air. We throw a local ecosystem out of balance, rendering it unfriendly to the food webs we rely on to survive and thrive. We filter for purity, and in doing so, leave ourselves weaker and more susceptible and frail. When we attempt to organize complex natural systems by simplifying them, we reduce the benefits gained from and the structural integrity of those systems.

Biologically, this is something we've done to ourselves for ages. And we've only recently been able to paint a more complete picture of why.

A microbiome is a complex community made up of microbiota—bacteria, fungi, archaea—that themselves make up larger, more complex organisms. The human microbiome, for instance, consists of only about 25 percent human genetic material, while the rest is made up of other wee-beasties. The creature we call a human being is partially its own genetically isolated entity, but it would be more correct to view each one of us as an ecosystem of interrelated pieces, much like a rainforest or coral reef. This fungus feeds these bacteria, which in turn helps this human cell process energy, and so on.

What we perceive to be a complete, seamless, thinking human is in fact a web of creatures, all of which have their own isolated genetic structures we can map and identify. And these non-human creatures outnumber the human parts three to one. A collection of purely human cells would not result in a fully functioning human.

An environmental biome, like that of a rainforest, is thrown completely out of whack when any part of it disappears, and sometimes with catastrophic consequences.

A simple, real-world example of this was seen in 1995 by a marine research vessel studying sardine populations off the coast of Southern California. The vessel found that the entire upper-ocean ecosystem was crippled due to a very small change in the water temperature in the area: only about 2 or 3 degrees Fahrenheit over the course of the 43 years in which they'd been keeping track.

The temperature difference between the water near the ocean floor and the water near the surface is usually large enough to cause the lower waters to continuously churn toward the surface, to the top of the so-called water column. That up-flowing water brings to the surface nutrients contained in the dead creature bits that settle on the ocean floor. Those nutrients are then gobbled up by phytoplankton, which in turn are eaten by zooplankton, which themselves are eaten by small fish, like sardines.

The biologists on this particular vessel found that the phytoplankton population had dropped by 80 percent in the past four decades, which in turn had caused a 30 percent drop in the sardine population. The creatures that fed on the sardines, like sea birds, had fared even worse, losing 90 percent of their number in less than a decade.

This die-off in these populations had been triggered by a small shift in the average water temperature. When that water column activity was disrupted, so were the populations of creatures located across the local food web.

Looking at the natural world in simplistic terms, it's easy to assume we're better off when things are simpler and more manageable.

Early agricultural techniques often involved the complete destruction of all plants that competed with whatever we were growing. More modern, sustainable techniques, on the other hand, recognize the value of mixing many types of plants together, which allows them to benefit from their interrelationships. This plant attracts this type of bug, which kills these other bugs which try to eat this plant, while the roots of this other plant share its nutrients with a nearby plant that has trouble doing so by itself.

Across much of the developed world, the large-scale, mono-plant agricultural approach still dominates. This approach requires vast quantities of fertilizers and equipment to maintain. It's an industry that fights against balance for the sake of purity, and in doing so tends to be far less sustainable, causing fields to go fallow for lack of nutrients, and entire ecosystems in the surrounding landscape to go bust as a result of its destructive chemicals and methods.

That balance can be more beneficial and sustainable than purity is not a new idea, but it is one that's relatively new to mainstream discussion and understanding in Western culture.

Our history is paved with purification efforts. Sometimes the targets are our systems, sometimes our genetics, sometimes our methods of education. These efforts always make sense, in the moment, to the contemporary people who are instigating them.

The people who want to enforce one set of standards for all schools, for instance, truly want to ensure that no child is left behind, and that everyone starts out with the same level and quality of education. Those who wanted to prevent the mentally or physically handicapped and the impoverished from reproducing merely wanted to ensure that subsequent generations didn't start out with genetic or social disadvantages.

Eugenics, the practice of preventing some groups from reproducing in order to "purify" the human race, has been dismissed as outdated hokum by most serious people these days. Sometimes this dismissal is for moral reasons, as it's fairly monstrous, by today's standards, to decide who can and cannot have kids. But it's also been left behind because we now know that part of what allows a species to survive and evolve is our ability to develop beneficial mutations, which are filtered out by genetics-based programs that would "purify" us. These mutations are not always immediately recognizable as such, but history has shown that species which fail to mutate also fail to survive changes to their environment. They lack the ability to adjust as the world adjusts around them.

Mono-curriculum school programs are still very much in vogue around the world, though they fall prey to many of the same weaknesses as eugenics. They disincentivize the emergence of beneficial mutations, which in turn keeps us from rapidly evolving our educational systems.

In the United States, for instance, we have a set of public schools that we try to hold to standards set by a group of people high up in the education system. Top-down management may make us feel better, because it ensures we have someone to blame if things go wrong, but it often represents an attempt to purify, rather than encouraging a diversity of teaching methods to spring up and flourish. Allowing different educational systems within the same country would be a politically volatile choice, as it would inherently result in some schools doing better than others in the short-term. But over time, it would also mean we'd have a far larger number of options to choose from, each potentially successful according to a different set of metrics. We'd also have a far larger body of data from which to pull.

We may find that some students do better under a creativity focused system being used in Detroit, while others really open up and reach their full potential under a stricter, test-oriented system based in Atlanta, while still others really seem to work well within a homework-less framework developed in Des Moines.

Mono-culture, mono-approach, or mono-species systems allow us to feel like we're purifying or simplifying a process, when in reality we're impeding potentially valuable mutations from occurring. Mutations that would help us evolve faster, be it biologically or socially.

Our purification predisposition operates on the individual level as well.

When we're presented with tools that give us auto-pedagogical super powers, we tend to use those tools, not to introduce ourselves to more and unfamiliar ideas, but to finely focus our attention on data that support our existing perspectives.

A "filter bubble" is not a physical thing, nor is it the product of just one app or website or operating system. The filter bubble that surrounds each of us is made up of algorithms, search results, activity tracking cookies, and the personal biases these tools amplify.

These technologies, in isolation, are each intended to fulfill specific purposes. Many of these purposes are helpful in some way—to us and to the companies providing them. We like to see news and images relevant to the people and things we're most interested in, so when Facebook shows us more articles shared by those people, and more videos and images related to the brands we like best, we're more likely to spend time on their site and with their apps interacting within their ecosystem. This, in turn, provides them with more clicks, which results in more ad revenue. It's seemingly win-win, but when combined with algorithms that determine our search results, and those that decide which headlines we see when we visit a news site, we start to run into problems.

The combination of these technologies, each of them intent on serving us better while also perpetuating their business models, results in our seeing the world through a distorted lens. We see a world that is relevant to us, that is shaped by our biases, which in turn makes us feel comfortable and engaged.

The impact of this is immense. None of these services or apps want to make you uncomfortable, and consequently they avoid making you feel any cognitive dissonance; any intellectual discomfort.

Cognitive dissonance is part of how we learn new things. If we grow up believing that Santa is real, learning that he's not can be disorienting and uncomfortable. So much of what we'd thought and done in the past was predicated on the idea that this jolly old elf was an actual person.

The same can be true of any type of information, whether it relates to our views on religion or politics, culture or literature, our friends' personalities or significant others' predilections.

Having your worldview shattered is uncomfortable and potentially debilitating, especially when we learn something that indicates we've been acting upon faulty information. But it's also the only way to become better informed and evolve our perspectives. Experiencing cognitive dissonance is the only way we grow and become better informed, our opinions predicated on more accurate information, rather than outdated beliefs or prejudices.

Filter bubbles are the ideological equivalent of mono-species agriculture or human eugenics programs. They have the best of intentions, especially on a granular, individual level. Pieces of these ideas can make sense and seem justifiable. When they're made into larger, actionable concepts, however, they often become harmful, and even devastating, to growth and change.

Filter bubbles aren't novel in human society. Sometimes they take the shape of repressive governmental regimes that demand everyone toe the line when it comes to official party doctrine. Sometimes they look more like an enclosed academic space, in which the theoretical is amplified at the expense of practical, real-world issues. Sometimes a person's filter bubble is the small town or small-minded family they grow up in, and their only exposure to the world, to ideas from outside, are glimpses caught on television or in books smuggled from the library and hidden in their locker at school.

Like with so many things, our bubble-building capabilities have been dramatically enhanced over the past few decades.

Our ability to reach out and get any information we might want to access today is unparalleled in human history. That our bubbles shape this information is a hindrance, but it's not an insurmountable barrier.

These bubbles are very real, but still poppable, provided we're able to recognize them for what they are: barriers between us and reality. Barriers that keep us from the information we require to make better-informed decisions and to become more refined versions of ourselves.

If there's one thing humans are good at, it's leaping over hurdles, knocking down walls, and figuring out ways to get to things we desire. Our self-made bubbles and boundaries are a major challenge today, and are unlikely to go away completely any time soon. But I'm bullish that we'll continue to innovate our way past the consequences of our prior innovations.

Meaning

We all find meaning in different things. As such, discussing meaning in any productive way can be a cumbersome undertaking. That said, there are two main types of meaning I want to address in this chapter.

The first is significance meaning. That is, imbuing moments or events with implicit substance so that, to us at least, there is more to them than meets the eye.

A chance glance from a stranger on the subway, or the sequence of lucky numbers in our fortune cookie being the same as our high school locker combination can both seem loaded with meaning. These are not coincidences, we think. What are the chances of something like that happening, after all? They are significant in some way, and it makes sense, from that perspective, to want to figure out how.

Most people, it should be noted, are terrible at offhandedly understanding, or even estimating, probability. You'd be a killjoy to deflate a friend who's erupting with enthusiasm over the perceived significance of receiving his old locker combination as a set of lucky numbers in a fortune cookie, but you'd be right in recognizing that although the chance of something like that happening is small, it's not beyond the realm of possibility. Unlikely things happen all the time. If something has a one in one-billion chance of happening, well, do you know how many things are happening at all times, to all of the over seven-billion people who live on the planet today? Our perception of how likely these events might be remains unchanged, because we see the world through the lens of a single individual. But if you do the math on that scale, it quickly becomes clear that the unlikely is actually not all that unlikely.

We also tend to notice and remember things we perceive to be unlikely more than things we don't perceive to be in any way unusual, even if those ignored things are, in fact, the less likely, more impressive, and more interesting happenstances.

This tendency to pay more attention to the seemingly unlikely events that happen to and around us is called "selective attention." Our brains have a bias toward patterns, and ignore so-called uninteresting data—things we are not primed to perceive as significant to us—and to put increased emphasis on the opposite, storing seemingly meaningful happenings more firmly in our memory. As a result, we're more likely to recall the times when the tarot card reader was right, and to completely forget or disregard the times when she was wrong. The significance of that card reader's words, then, elevate in our mind, while the significance of information we might read about the practice of tarot card reading having no basis in reality and no scientific credibility, decreases.

This is part of why, too, we tend to underestimate just how likely seemingly unlikely events might be. Our brains latch on to the amazingness of this chance reappearance of old, familiar numbers, while dismissing other bits of data—it wasn't on your fortune cookie, but on your friend's, two of the numbers were rearranged, you've been going to that same Chinese food place for five years, and never before received a familiar set of numbers inside your cookie—which in turn results in our finding meaning in what is almost certainly meaningless. The part-time worker or machine algorithm that jots those numbers down on the fortune cookie papers most likely is not a wizard, and it's far more likely that the familiarity and feeling of significance is merely the consequence of our brains wigging out over the perceived connection, due to its pattern-finding predilections. Because that's what it does.

Why are our brains so primed for patterns?

As with so many things brain-related, we can't say with absolute certainty, but there is a good argument to be made that this pattern-seeking habit is what allows us to think, interact, and build tools.

A creature who is able to piece together a sequence of events can infer causality—that other beast over there drank from the water, and now it's dead, so perhaps I shouldn't drink that water—and benefit from that perception. A creature who can recognize cause and effect while extrapolating further, imagining how things might be changed, can manipulate the world around them. That is, they wouldn't just avoid the water that seems to be killing other animals, they might be able to figure out new ways to get water, by folding large leaves to collect dew and rainwater. The idea to use leaves as collection tools, by the way, would also be the result of observation and pattern detection: watching the rain drip down the leaves, and the dew accumulate on the leaves each morning, would lead to the conclusion that these green things are related to this free-flowing water somehow, and could perhaps be manipulated to sate our thirst.

The Baader-Meinhof Phenomenon, also called the "frequency illusion," is relevant to this discussion. This is a phenomenon that you've almost certainly experienced at some point in your life: you buy a new car, let's say a Saturn coupe, and then suddenly, from the next day onward, you see Saturn coupes absolutely everywhere. It's as if the entire world is copying you. There can't have been this many Saturn coupes on the road before you bought yours; you've never seen so many of them out in the world before. How strange and coincidental.

Of course, this is neither strange nor coincidental. It's the consequence of your brain earmarking a new bit of information as important. This brand and type of car is something that you've been thinking about and now own. It's important to be able to pick out your own car from all the cars in a parking lot, but it's also a shape that you now recognize, a logo that you've come to know, and a collection of design elements that you now see more clearly in a crowd of other, less-vital-seeming car-mounted design elements. These other Saturn coupes were always there in your environment, but now that they seem important to your brain, you'll notice them more frequently, and remember noticing them, because that perceived significance is amplified, collected as relevant data.

The fortune cookie, the sudden appearance of cars like your own—neither are mystical or magical. The word "synchronicity" was coined by Carl Jung to describe such things, and to justify the paranormal nature they certainly had, when in reality he merely lacked the clarity afforded by modern brain and social sciences.

That said, something not being inherently magical doesn't mean it isn't important. It doesn't mean such things can't be vital as mental milestones or as valuable intellectual footnotes.

Finding significance in things that are not significant is what causes a lot of us to have harmful beliefs that hold us back in many ways, but it's also kind of a super power that provides us with ambitions. It can bring out the best in us. Or rather, it can help us bring out the best in ourselves.

This is the second type of meaning I mentioned. The first is significance we imbue in an event or object that makes that thing or happenstance seem more important than it is. The second is the type of meaning we pursue throughout our lives. The sort of meaning that, in a lot of cases, provides us with the intellectual and emotional will to make it through tough times and to work hard toward something big, something larger than ourselves.

In some cases, this meaning takes the shape of religion, or of a particular brand of governance, or of one's own family and their well-being. Sometimes it's the wholehearted pursuit of knowing the unknown, or taking down the wicked, or teaching things you believe should be more widely known.

There are as many meaningful pursuits as there are people, and although we have no reason to believe that any such meaning is divine or magical, that doesn't diminish the potential benefits of finding meaning, perhaps even multiple sources of it, throughout our lives.

People who feel they have purpose tend to live longer. People who have convictions, who believe something to be not just true, but important, have a greater capacity to endure discomfort, pain, and antipathy from those who believe differently. People who ascribe some type of meaning to the work they do or the goals they're pursuing are more likely to see the journey as the point of the exercise, rather than seeing life as a necessary period of suffering on the way to a goal they hope to reach someday. The journey itself is meaningful. The goal is important, but the act of working toward it, even when painful or disheartening, is meaningful by association.

When we talk about "finding meaning" in our lives, this is the type of meaning we're usually discussing. Very seldom does someone hope to find meaning in the sense of recognizing more cars like the one she just bought on the road, or finding familiarity in the lucky numbers contained within the folds of a fortune cookie.

But these types of meaning are inextricably connected. The pattern-seeking portions of our brains make connections and assume relationships between things, and it's those same neurons, those same interconnections between memory and higher-reasoning and animal instinct and whatever it is that makes us feel conscious that allow us to feel a sense of not just existence, but purpose. They allow us to see the act of feeding the hungry as not just one more action among all the actions we perform every day, but something significant.

If we feed this person, they will feel something, and hopefully something better than they feel now. Some of the fear and desperation will disappear, and they may have more capacity for joy. Beyond that, they'll go on to live their own lives, full of the same tribulations we all face, but also packed with moments of happiness resulting from goals accomplished, the joy of relationships, and the thrill of new discoveries. And by giving this person something to eat, we've played some small role in that. We have in some small way served as a catalyst for all that emotion, all those feelings, all that experience, all that life.

Without the sometimes overenthusiastic pattern-recognition tendencies of our brains, we would be unable to make these connections, and feeding a stranger would be just one more act, with no more significance than brushing our teeth or driving to work or feeding ourselves an unremarkable lunch. The cause and effect assumption would be lost, and our ability to dig deeper and subconsciously guess at what this action of ours might mean, not just for us, but for others, perhaps many others, would not exist.

The world, lacking this meaning that we generate, would be a much flatter, more pragmatic place, I think. That's assuming we were able to build such a world to begin with, which is anything but certain. I'm guessing that much of the human desire to explore would be lost, due to the lack of imagination about what we might find over the next horizon. As a result, we'd probably never have evolved and spread out the way we did, and would not have had the same biological inclination toward tool usage and brain development.

I also have trouble imagining what would drive us to do anything beyond the bare basics under such circumstances. It seems unlikely we'd feel incentivized to achieve anything more than the essentials that would allow us to survive another day. We'd have little reason to believe investment in infrastructure or assets would pay off, and we'd have little reason to make small sacrifices for the greater good of the family, tribe, society, or species. We wouldn't be able to perceive any significance in those actions, and as such, the frantic, genetic-level drive toward self-preservation would be the only thing keeping us going.

There are many causes out there that are misguided and faulty and based on false-premises. I think we're sometimes too dependent on gut-instincts when we should think analytically, and put too much faith in incomplete mental models when we should trust our gut. We adhere to ideologies dogmatically, assuming that the meaning found within them is the only possible meaning and the only possible source of valid morality. We misunderstand coincidences, seeing them either as messages from the sky or remarkable impossibilities, ignoring the truly remarkable things that happen around us all day, every day. Among the remarkable things we often misunderstand or ignore is the incredible persistence of a species that has the capacity to both extrapolate and care.

The pursuit of meaning, of significance, is a valid one. It's valuable and, wherever we find it, it tends to be more asset than liability.

But it's also worth being conscious of where this feeling

comes from. We are the ones who imbue things with significance. We don't discover significant things, we discover things and make them significant. Recognizing and remembering this allows us to better understand and interact with people who find meaning in different places than we do. It also allows us to find meaning in many and varied things.

Balance

When wielding a weapon, be it a sword or a quarterstaff or a semiautomatic pistol, one of the most important properties to check is how it rests in your hands.

Does it wobble? Is it overbalanced to the front, or the pommel? When you swing the sword, does it pull you from your feet? Does the gun kick too far in an awkward direction, pulling your aim from your target?

A weapon can be effective whether or not it's well-balanced. You can cut someone's head off with a sword even if that sword pulls you off your feet as you swing.

But there are key, vital moments when we come to appreciate balance. In the case of armed combat, it's when an assailant is swinging some kind of weapon back at us, or parrying, or dodging with a followup attack. If we're off balance in these moments, we'll find ourselves exposed, our counterattack hindered, our lives on the line.

But balance is not only a concern for samurai, cowboys, and soldiers. The metaphor of weaponry is apt because it provides a dramatic visual for the idea of pushing too hard, and in doing so exposing oneself to threats that could have otherwise been easily handled. An overenthusiastic swing with a blade-heavy sword means we can't quickly pull that blade back up, post swing, to defend ourselves. But an over-focus on a single aspect of our lives, some attribute or proficiency, without a similar focus on a counterbalance for it, can leave us exposed to non-weapon-related threats. It can ruin plans and disrupt ambitions.

More than once I've fallen prey to the siren's call of unbalance. After university I ran a branding studio in Los Angeles, and invested a great deal of time and energy in ensuring my practice grew each month. My focus on this allowed me to make a great deal of money and attain a large amount of professional prestige in a relatively short amount of time, but I did so at the expense of essentially everything else in my life. My hobbies shriveled from lack of attention. My relationships suffered, as I had little time to interact with my significant other, much less go out with her. My health was being hammered, as I subsisted on whatever I could grab before or after long meetings with clients and marathon work sessions that would last late into the night. I would then collapse into bed for a few hours of sleep before hauling myself out of it early the next morning before anyone else was awake so I could scrape together a few more hours of productivity before any of my clients started calling.

I had swung hard, imbuing my weapon with a lot of might and accuracy, but in doing so had thrown everything else wildly off-balance. My stance was in ruin, my weak spots were exposed. If this doesn't work, I often thought to myself, I'm screwed. There's nothing else. Everything else has been given up for this.

This brand of mono-focus is revered by Western society, as it implies dedication and a singular purpose. We celebrate the earning of money, the accumulation of prestige in one's field, the production of grand works, and the respect of one's peers.

But what we sometimes fail to notice is that many of our heroes who succeed by these standards are two-dimensional creatures. If you look at them straight on from the right direction, they seem larger than life. But if you take a step to the side, you see that they lack depth or density. They disappear completely. They are non-entities by any other metric of success.

Balance, in this sense, doesn't necessarily imply involvement with numerous clubs and an interest in many hobbies. It doesn't mean you have a large group of friends and are well-read. It doesn't mean anything in particular, in fact. There are no specifics of that kind to be found in this term.

What it does mean is that rather than allowing one or just a few things to throw you off balance, you have different things in your life—different activities, different people, different interests—which exercise a push-pull effect on each other.

There's nothing inherently unhealthy about working long hours, or working hard on something you care about or think will benefit you in the long term. It only becomes potentially harmful when in doing so you neglect other aspects of your life that require attention. When you start to lose density and become less three-dimensional.

Balance is vital for individuals, but it's also an important consideration for groups. And imbalance within societies can take several different forms.

It can manifest as an unhealthy fixation on a few values at the expense of all others. It can result from a focus on monoculture or "purity" in genetics or ideology. It can emerge from traditionalism and a lack of understanding of the current larger context. And it can stem from an internal lack of structural integrity.

When a society holds up two or three values as the most vital, the most important, to the point that they outshine all others, it can diminish the stability of that culture.

The United States is many things to many people, for instance, and it is this way because it represents different flavors of freedom, a particular type of capitalism, the ability to express oneself with words or art, access to certain types of infrastructure and resources, exposure to many different types of ideas and people, and relative safety provided by a variety of security-focused systems. If the US were to rebrand, however, and become just the land of this one specific flavor of capitalism, and all those other things are given up so we can bolster this one idea, really become gung-ho about just the economic side of things, a small niche of people would be very excited. But everyone else, the people who have lost so many other liberties and benefits, would be horrified. Yes, that one thing is beneficial alongside all the other things, the other foundational cornerstones that have made the country what it is today. But in isolation, no single one of these focuses is sufficient to create a well-balanced country. A larger, wider, more diverse foundation makes anything you build atop it more stable. No one wants to live in an inverted pyramid. You want the majority of the substance at the bottom of the structure.

Throughout history we've witnessed many concerted efforts to "purify" cultures. Sometimes this has been through ideological witch hunts, like the Red Scare, during which society was flogged into a frenzy by Joseph McCarthy and his ilk, and during the literal witch hunt that took place around Europe and in New England here in the US.

We've also seen attempts to "purify" at a genetic-level, with groups culling what came to be labeled "undesirable" traits and lineages, as when the Nazis decided to kill off Jews, Roma, non-whites of all heritages, homosexuals, and anyone else they considered to be impure, in the Teutonic, Hitlerite sense of the word.

Many other countries, including the United States, have had their own eugenics programs, through which they tried to accomplish the same ends. But instead of using death camps, they sterilized the poor, the mentally handicapped, the diseased, and people from groups that were at the time considered to be "less than" by mainstream society. It's fortunate that efforts of this kind did not go further than relatively small experimental trials, outside of Third Reich-era Germany. Not only would it have been devastating to the groups that were being victimized by these efforts, but it also would have left the human race frailer as a consequence.

Genetic diversity, as we've learned in the years since then, is what makes an ecosystem strong and resilient. A world populated by blonde-haired, blue-eyed Aryans would have been aesthetically pleasing to the Nazis, but would have been weak to diseases and environmental changes. The larger the genetic pool, the stronger the species, because that species is more likely to have, somewhere, in someone, the resistance needed to fend off a plague, or the skin tone necessary to survive and thrive in a new geography. Balance, in this case, means variety, even if that variety isn't always initially appreciated.

Another common type of societal imbalance stems from a fixation on the past at the expense of the present, which leads to a truncation of options in the future.

We have a bias toward conservatism. That's not a political statement, it's a sociological one. We, as humans, are predisposed to favor things that already exist, which shape the status quo. When new technologies change how society operates, we are, on average, biased against these new technologies because we would rather have the devil we know than the demon we don't yet fully understand.

Autonomous cars are a contemporary example of this. The technologies required to make self-driving cars a reality have developed rapidly over the last several decades, and have recently come to fully functioning fruition. Several companies already have their own autonomous cars on the road, and the failure rate of these cars is far lower than that of human drivers. Yet, when an autonomous car is involved in an accident, even if the accident is not the fault of the software, but another driver behaving erratically, the majority of the headlines the next day will be about how this new technology isn't ready, and that we probably shouldn't trust this technology, ever.

Not all new technologies are ready for mainstream use and not all technologies should be implemented at all. But a bias toward traditions and the familiar keeps us from developing solutions to old problems as quickly as we might. Imbalances occur naturally as complex systems degrade over time, and the only way to counter this degradation is to consistently introduce new stabilizing structures.

Finally, many societies become imbalanced because of a lack of stability within their very framework.

This is, in general, less a problem on the broader scale, as most national governments have a large number of systems and rules and structures in place that keep the sky from falling when something goes awry. If the unlikely occurs, chances are someone has war-gamed it already and worked out a step-by-step manual for how to understand what's happening, get the necessary facts, and take action in a way that results in the least possible devastation.

But this isn't necessarily the case for smaller groups of people, like neighborhoods or school districts, and isn't always the case for nascent nations and newborn governments. There have been many historical, and some quite recent, instances of well-meaning revolutionaries ousting their leader, only to have the military step in to take over, post-coup. This isn't just because the military has more guns; it's because the military has a more stable structure, a tradition of discipline, and systems in place to help it manage something as complex as a nation. The revolutionaries, had they more balance, more of a focus on governing and managing rather than simply developing ideas, might have a better chance of not just taking, but holding and maintaining the country they care about. But because of that mono-purpose, that fixation that makes them so effective at one thing, at tearing something down, they also often lack the capability to do the opposite. As such, even a relatively mediocre—but mediocre in a balanced way—military takeover is more likely to work than rule by a group of well-meaning but imbalanced rebels.

One way to achieve balance on a personal level is to take a step back and take a good, long look at your own life. What are you focused on right now? What do you wish you had more time and energy for? What weaknesses do you see in yourself, be they habitual, skill-based, or part of what makes you, you? Are you quick to anger? Slow to decide? Are you great at programming, but terrible at communicating? Are you kicking ass at work, but failing as a spouse? Or perhaps you're doing splendidly as a friend to those who are important in your life, but lack professional purpose or success? Maybe you lack a basic level of monetary stability which, if you had it, might make you feel less stressed and worried all the time?

A focus on balance doesn't mean a focus on anything specific. Your priorities completely depend on you, where you are now, and where you want to be. It's a matter of filling in the gaps, strengthening the weak spots, and doing your best to ensure you're not a two-dimensional person. It's attempting to be more round and fulfilled, rather than flat, flawed-feeling, and structurally vulnerable.

On the personal level and on the societal level, this isn't a one-step process. It's a journey that doesn't end. It's not a punch, it's a posture held and adjusted over time to achieve the best possible shape for who you want to be.

Explore & Exploit

There is a latent push-pull between the drive to explore and the drive to exploit. There are internal mechanisms that prod us toward one extreme or the other, and this balance tilts differently at different periods in our lives: the conflict between progress and conservation is not a modern invention.

Like with so many things, though, the ideal balance between them seems to be just that: balance. Extreme positions in either direction leave us more fragile than if we were somewhere closer to the middle. Unfortunately, the framing of this conflict in the public sphere all too often portrays it as zero-sum, and doesn't leave room for compromise.

We're told we must choose. Are you in favor of progress or conservation? Do you want to push boundaries, or defend them? Do you want to see change, or do you want to prevent it?

Politics taints this topic before we're ever able to have an honest discussion about it. Most political processes are, in fact, zero-sum, where you either win or lose, with no in-between, and consequently the perception of what it means to be "conservative" or "progressive" has been flattened. We're offered two starkly oppositional options and nothing in between, because the parties on either end tell us it is so. In practice this means we have few realistic political choices, because the polarized ends of the spectrum control the resources, the conversation, and sometimes even the legal capability to participate in the system.

This is a shame. Few of us, I think, are absolutists in anything, much less the overall scaffolding upon which our worldviews are built. Yes, we are increasingly, passively manipulated by those who hope to sway us toward their ideologies, toward checking the box next to the name of their candidate in the next election, or toward their preferred philosophical cause, or their brand of laundry detergent. We face a constant intellectual assault from all sides. But although these forces are quite powerful, they don't completely dilute who we are on a more fundamental level. I may be convinced that this political party represents my views, or that associating myself with this brand of swimwear is consistent with my allegiance to a particular social group. But it's unlikely I'll change absolutely everything about myself because I listen to a polarized talk radio station, or am exposed to a sequence of well-placed commercial jingles.

This is not to understate the potential power of these messages: they are, in fact, immensely influential. We're generally not aware of just how much our views are shaped by these messages until we attempt to explain our position in specifics. Particularly for those not super-involved in politics, it's remarkable how quickly seemingly logical answers give way to party slogans and PR-friendly talking points. Our thoughts are not always our own, because when we don't have strong opinions about something, we adopt the ideas of others as a stopgap solution.

If I don't have a detailed understanding of a particular trade deal, it makes sense that I would look to an expert on the topic for more information. I choose which expert to listen to based on their affiliations: perhaps they're presented as an expert by the party I tend to agree with more frequently. As a result, I now hold an opinion that I don't fully understand, or which is dependent on details I haven't noticed or can't comprehend, and which was provided to me by a political organization that doesn't necessarily align with me on every particular. There's a decent chance, then, that a substantial portion of what I think I know is, in fact, more heavily slanted than I suspected. This trade deal, perhaps, is not good for people like me and my priorities, but rather for people who are involved with and influential within the party in which I've put my trust.

This is something that everyone—even clever political insiders and the marketing minds behind the jingles that sell you soap—fall prey to. In a past life, I built brands that were meant to tell a certain story, in the hopes of evoking a response from people who wanted to be associated with that type of tale. If you present as a company that is all about adventure, being a weekend warrior, and leaving the trail to blaze your own, then you'll be attractive to people who see themselves that way, or who want to see themselves that way, and who assume that by buying products from a company that has strongly associated itself with those ideas, they too will be associated with those concepts.

We proudly wear logos because we believe they say something about us. The concepts imbued in those brands are shared with those of us who slap them on our shirts or bags or sunglasses or laptops. Even as someone who built such brands and who understands how they work, and all the tricks that are used to communicate them, both overtly and subtly, I still fall prey to them. I still feel more strongly about some brands than others because of the story they tell, not just because of the product they sell.

These are immensely influential messages we're surrounded by essentially all the time. The research on how many marketing messages we're exposed to each day is fuzzy, as it's tricky to suss out just what "exposure" means, and the number of such messages varies wildly depending on where you live, what you do each day, and so on. We're prone to filtering for the things in our environments that are most relevant to us and our needs, so chances are, if you and I walked down the same street at the same time, we'd notice different messages, consciously and subconsciously. I might not notice a flashy ad for a car, for instance, because I'm not particularly interested in cars, and as such, those ads, and others using the same aesthetics—a lot of ads for clubs and alcoholic products use similar photography and typography—blend in to the background for me. The opposite may be true for you: those car ads may be exciting and interesting, while the aged sign for the used bookstore that pops out to me goes completely unnoticed by you.

These messages are visuals and audio, they move and hold still, they flutter around and shout for attention, and they wait calmly, placidly, certain we'll come to them. Some of these messages we'd recognize as ads, and sometimes they cross the line into wholesale propaganda. Some are subtle and innocuous, and even if we paid close attention, we might not notice that the character in that show we like is wearing a particular brand of watch. When we're exposed to that same style of timepiece later on, we won't know why, but we'll ascribe to it certain properties, as that subconscious association with the character from the show will carry over to real life.

Most of the messages we encounter each day are developed and presented very intentionally: usually to encourage us to buy something, either immediately or at some point in the future.

In some cases, the "buying" is actually "buying into." Perhaps they're selling us on a belief system or religion, or maybe a political party or stance on a particular law.

Frighteningly few of these messages incentivize us to step back, take a deep breath, and thoroughly consider an issue. It's a rare political advertisement that tells us, "There is no absolute right answer to this question, and no absolute right position to take. We and our opponents in this matter are both right for different reasons. It's up to you to determine where you stand by educating yourself on the subject, and understanding as completely as possible which choice most closely aligns with your philosophical priorities. Vote yes or no: it's the process that matters."

You won't see that ad, but it's the truth, isn't it? When, in the history of politics, has something been presented that's been absolutely right or wrong for every single person?

In response to that question, partisan feelings may bubble to the surface. "Surely," you might be thinking, "this position on health care is right for everyone. I wouldn't support it if it wasn't. Anyone who votes against it is voting against their own interests."

That may be true, to some degree. But consider that there's always a winner and a loser with such positions, and it may be that the loser is some large, corporate entity. I'm not trying to say that it's right or wrong to support or oppose efforts to empower such entities. But I am saying efforts in favor of such groups make just as much rational sense, for some people, and the groups they are a part of, as efforts to disempower them. To say, then, that a given policy or political position or law is right for everyone is almost certainly incorrect. Our politics are defined, in part, by the oppositional stances of the political parties involved. It would be difficult to find a political party that makes decisions that don't favor someone, even if it doesn't always favor who they claim it does.

The conflict between explore and exploit, between progress and conservation, is an important one to understand. Seeing how it connects our politics, and to the overwhelming number of marketing messages around us, makes us more capable of striking a balance, rather than falling prey to the forces of extremism and polarization.

One uncomfortable truth that can be difficult to acknowledge is that we need both ends of this spectrum. As individuals and societies, we would be worse off if we lost either side.

Exploration is what exposes us to new ideas and allows us to grow and evolve. It's often uncomfortable and difficult, and there is value in the frictions the explorer encounters along the way. Exploration helps us understand when we're wrong and forces us to reconsider. It helps us understand that absolutes are rare, if they exist at all, and that there are people in the world with different perspectives and needs. We can argue in favor of our position, but exploration helps us realize that ours is just one of many.

Conservation is what allows us to maintain, defend, and exploit that which we've already collected and accomplished. It's what helps us build atop lessons already learned, and what ensures the streets are clean and the electrical grid continues churning out energy. Conservative ideas are what allow us to feel like part of a larger whole, and to understand who we are and why we do what we do. It's about predictability and comfort. It's about security and having a tribe.

Progressives are more capable of doing their job when there's a solid, stable surface under their feet. Historically, many of the greatest explorers have been from well-conserved, well-established cultures that built up stockpiles and resiliencies that allowed them to send ambassadors out into the world. These cultures were able to take these risks because they knew that even if their efforts failed, the majority of people were still well taken care of.

Conservatives need progressives because without them, the predictable and stable status quo they build and defend becomes, over time, less stable and less defensible. Rigidity leads to cracks, no matter how sturdy the construction, and the only viable method of keeping such structures from crumbling is maintaining malleability that allows it to bend when it would otherwise break. Explorers bring home treasures—new ideas, new people, new flavors, new music and artifacts and everything else—for the tribe to enjoy. This enriches the existing collective, and allows them to benefit from the ideas, inventions, and perspectives of others, without the whole population needing to go out and expose themselves to risk.

Striking a balance between these oppositional viewpoints is the most ideal situation, if we can manage it. There is a latent, perhaps biological difficulty inherent in this, because those who prefer novelty to stability tend to be dismissive of conservative ideals, while those who romanticize tribal structure and consistency over the unpredictability and unknowns of progress have trouble understanding why they would want to risk what they've got to integrate novelty.

This mutual distaste and discord is amplified by politics, and especially modern politics, which have increasingly powerful, effective tools at their disposal when making their case. Very often, when making their arguments, they also take the opportunity to paint the opposition with unfavorable colors.

One of the strengths of governmental systems that allow disagreement is that we tend to end up somewhere in the middle much of the time. If we push too far in either direction, we actually weaken our structure, and end up with a more fragile, frail system than we might otherwise have. Passionate voices on all sides, rational arguments made by people with differing viewpoints, and approximately the same amount of power held by diverse people who disagree about a great number of things, are all requisites of a strong, resilient democracy.

Many democratic systems, unfortunately, have become less about finding ideal middle-grounds and more about winning at all costs. It's not enough anymore to have the better idea: you must destroy the opposition by smearing their people and misrepresenting their arguments, using cowardly non-arguments, emotionally manipulative non-issues, and in some cases, outright lies.

It's hard to say how we step back from this precipice, as there aren't many historical examples to learn from, and certainly none that take place in a society as interconnected as ours.

One of the fundamental challenges we'll face in the coming years, I think, will be figuring out how to have conversations, not just about the dichotomy of explore and exploit, but about anything and everything. How to have discussions about important things and relatively mundane things, and how we might have those conversations with a shared understanding that we're trying to achieve the same thing, even if that might not immediately appear to be the case.

Our current path isn't an absolute recipe for disaster, but it is a concoction that requires attention and participation, if we hope to keep it from smoldering into something unrecognizable, unpalatable, and lacking in substance.

Reality & Meta-Reality

To say that something is "meta" is to identify it as being outside and above the thing to which it's referring. Metaphysics is a branch of philosophy that wrangles with ideas beyond the physical, outside of what can be described and understood by physics. The search for meaning, for instance, or the attempt to comprehend whether there are forces beyond those we know and can scientifically demonstrate and support, like a god or spirits or ghosts, are metaphysical pursuits.

Meta-reality, then, is something that resides outside and above our general conception of what's real and true. There's the concrete world in which we live, in which we perceive a physical existence, and in which our social structures and commonly shared ideals reside. The cars we drive are a part of our reality, and so are the traffic laws that help us get from point A to point B in those cars.

Those traffic laws, though, are not tangible realities, they're agreed-upon limitations to our actions which allow more of us, on average, to travel safely. You cannot pick up a law, nor can you destroy it. It's an idea we've made tangible through our common agreement to adhere to it; to enforce it. That it has come to seem real in the sense that it's written down on paper and if we ignore it there will be consequences, is a testament to our ability as imaginative creatures to make the incorporeal, physical. To adjust real-world, physical conditions in support of immaterial things.

Our ability to make ideas feel like things is part of what allows us to socialize, organize, and aggregate effort as a species. If we couldn't imagine laws as real, as things that are truly there, as opposed to nebulous things we can safely ignore, we'd have trouble building societal systems. That we can imagine relationships between ourselves and other people who are not genetic relatives is astounding. That we can imagine relationships between ourselves and other people who happen to have been born on the same parcel of land, separated from other parcels by imaginary borders, is nothing short of remarkable.

International borders, the invisible lines we draw between Us and Them, are meta-realities. There's nothing material about these borders—no natural law, like gravity, that determines where one country ends and another begins. When the Allies pulled the Ottoman Empire apart in the aftermath of World War I, they were not violating the laws of nature. The Ottoman Empire was never "real" in the same sense that a tree is real. People worldwide collectively imagined it was real, and acted as if it was real, and laws were enforced as if it was real, and people felt a kinship with others who lived within that broad swathe of land as if they had something in common, but these were not truths, not absolutes. An Ottoman was not an Ottoman in the same way that a rock is a rock.

These labels, and the perceptions that we have about these labels, are fabrications. It's nationalistic hand-waving that has meaning because we commonly agree it does. It stands to reason, then, that if we ever collectively agreed that it did not have this meaning, then it would not.

That's a wild idea, isn't it? That we could do away with national borders simply by deciding to?

Many things we perceive to be powerful, to be meaningful, are only so because we give them that power. We provide them with significance, and poof, they have it.

Christmas, as a holiday, is thought to have been established in the year 274 AD as a power-move by Emperor Aurelian of Rome, to counter the traditional Pagan festival, *Dies Natalis Solis Invicti*. That's one theory, but there are others.

Some faiths hold that Christmas should be celebrated on January 7, since that's when the date of December 25, measured using the historical Julian calendar, would fall when translated to the current, Gregorian calendar. There are other interpretations and writings that claim Jesus' birth, which is the supposed rationale for the holiday, actually took place sometime in March, or April, or May, or maybe November. There is little data to support any of these dates, which perhaps shouldn't be surprising since the date we're trying to calculate is the date a miracle—something metaphysical—occurred within the physical world. The premise itself is soft and prone to interpretation and bias.

Recognizing this muddle, though, is a great opportunity. It means that, because there's no truth to the matter, no facts to find, and because "truth" in this context is maybe an unknowable thing, we can make the truth whatever we want it to be.

If we're trying to decide when Christmas should take place, and there's no firm agreement about when it should take place based on historical data, and no real agreement as to what we're celebrating in the first place—a general celebration for a religious figure, a celebration of the exact date of his birth, a celebration of a season in which that birth supposedly took place, an appropriation of a historical festival

—we can move this celebration on the calendar, and change its shape, however we choose.

That means Christmas, in its current incarnation, needn't be celebrated on December 25. In some countries, and by some groups, it's already celebrated the day before or the day after or twelve days later. This is not a sacred thing. This is not a natural law, like gravity. Christmas as it's often presented is not a fundamental truth, it's a thing we made up and generally agreed upon. We could agree upon something different.

Why might we do this? Maybe to make room for other holidays during that time of year. Maybe to put an increased focus on secular New Year celebrations, so a broader swathe of humanity has something around which to unify and share. Maybe it would make sense as a business move: if we realize there's a massive downswing in sales in March, but there are sufficient other things happening at the end of the year to keep sales steady, we could move the official celebration of Christmas to the spring and balance our economic output.

There may never be an actionable reason to move Christmas, or to change it in any way beyond the normal, slow-and-steady evolutions that have already occurred.

But knowing we can, that this day we've chosen for this celebration is not actually special, is important. It's important we recognize that, by astronomical standards, there's nothing unique about December 25. It has sometimes, historically, been the day with the least amount of sunlight in the Northern Hemisphere. That's it. It was meaningful in that way, at some point, on some parts of the planet, but as a universal concept? In 2016, the Winter Solstice was on December 21, and you didn't see anyone outside a planetarium making a big deal about it.

We have the power to alter things, to change the way society operates, to decide which things we hold dear. We have the ability to rearrange traditions and shatter those that no longer serve us. If we wanted to, and if we decided it was necessary for some greater goal, we could get rid of Christmas and nothing bad would happen. The same religious concepts could be celebrated and held sacred in other ways. The same family-centric rituals could be conducted via other means, at other times. The world would not spin off its axis. The world, the physical world, that is, wouldn't even recognize this as a change; except, perhaps, in the sense that fewer resources were torn from the Earth and spun into consumer goods in the months leading up to the celebration. The landfills in the days following the event would be less full than usual.

I don't bring this up to trash Christmas. I enjoy the holiday, and most holidays, because they're excuses to stop and take note, to install new habits, to enjoy the company of friends and family. The more holidays the better.

And it can be a lot of fun when these holidays are connected to historical or quasi-historical events. Feeling like you're perpetuating something deep and meaningful adds spice to the ritual, and all the strange little colloquial add-ons change the flavor just enough that, if you tried, you could celebrate Christmas every year and never have the same holiday, twice.

We have the ability to create or destroy holidays as we see fit. We needn't have a government mandate to do so, though it certainly doesn't hurt in achieving rapid, widespread adoption. These events, these moments in time that we've delineated as important and reserved for certain types of merrymaking are not, unto themselves, special. They're days like any other day that we've pointed at and said, "On this one, we'll paint eggs and eat candy." And on another otherwise not-special day, we point and say, "On this one, we'll all buy explosives, fire them into the sky, and drink more beer than usual."

We could perform these same rituals on any other day, but by doing them together, at the same time, we reinforce our kinship. We take part in something bigger than ourselves.

There is significance in these days, not because there's anything special about the day itself, and not because the universe would notice if we decided not to have Christmas or Easter or the 4th of July or New Years this year. There's significance because we've created events around them. Our imaginations and collective willpower are sufficient to change the financial destiny of entire industries and countries, and the moods and habits of individuals around the world, by holding these events. We can make meaningless days meaningful, meaningless moments the most important moments of our lives, and meaningless creatures into best friends, be they humans or dogs or charming little lizards.

We can only do this optimally, though, if we recognize this power for what it is. If we can see ourselves living within imaginary systems that we've installed, sometimes intentionally and sometimes due to tradition or habit or because it was already happening and all we did was formalize it, then we can reshape our world, our calendar, our relationships, and the way we perceive ourselves and others. We can build more intentionally. We can celebrate with greater enthusiasm. We can rearrange things so that we don't enshrine the ignorance and prejudice and mistakes of the past, but instead learn from these things, take the good stuff, the valuable experiences and facts, and move forward. We can construct something us-shaped, something that looks like modern humanity with all its rich variety.

Being capable of differentiating between real and meta-real, between things that are concrete, and things that only seem to be because we agree to make them so, allows us to more easily sort the rigid from the changeable.

This doesn't mean our imagined realities, our traffic laws

and holidays, will necessarily be any easier to change than tangible realities, like rocks and gravity. But it does mean that we'll have a clearer understanding of how the former comes into being, what leads to their solidification, and how we might ensure these concepts, both existing and newly fabricated, remain malleable in the future.

Consistency

During the 2004 US Presidential election, the term "flip-flopper" emerged as an insult.

The machine behind George W. Bush outflanked the machine behind John Kerry in many ways, but that term was probably the most viral and hard to shake off. John Kerry, they claimed, was a flip-flopper. He didn't maintain a steady ideology. He changed his mind about things. How can you trust someone like that?

I remember, at that time, questioning the merit of this accusation. Why was it a bad thing to change your mind? Why, if you learned something new, would you not adjust your perspective and actions accordingly?

Politicians, of course, are not well-known for saying what they really believe. Even the ones who are known for "telling it like it is" are fed lines which may not ever intersect with their actual ideologies. But the idea that to change one's mind is a liability, not an asset, is chilling to me. That we would hold up "consistency at any cost" as valorous, rather than crippling, doesn't jibe with reality. It's not the strongest that survive, but those most adaptable to change. It's not the most rigid, but the most malleable.

Evoking evolutionary theory, of course, isn't always the best way to win elections, or hearts and minds. Stability and security tend to sell a lot better than possibility and dynamism, especially when the intended market is registered voters.

Consistency makes us feel comfortable. Being able to wake up each morning and know what's going to happen next satisfies the parts of our brain that look for patterns and seek understanding. Rituals and routines allow us to feel we understand what's happening, and why, and allow us to feel in control. It also keeps the scaredy-cat parts of our brain that stay alert for anything unfamiliar and unusual from freaking out all the time.

Rituals and routines allow us to feel comfortable and safe. And this is a disposition that is often amplified as we grow older. We transition from xenophiles, those who are attracted to the unknown, into xenophobes, those who are afraid of it. This isn't an absolute thing, of course, and some of us buck this trend. But in general we seek out novelty and strangeness when we're young, filling our brains with new information and perspectives, and our microbiota with unfamiliar, interesting bacteria and viruses, but harden as the years progress. We crystallize as people, and become more focused on nesting and defending what we've already got, rather than going out and finding new things to bring home.

There are many reasons for this shift. Biologically, we're prone to becoming less adventurous and more predictable in part because those are traits associated with good parenting. You're more likely to raise healthy youngsters if you're at home, taking care of things, than if you're out seeking new thrills. This absolutely isn't always the case, and many people maintain adventurous spirits while they raise kids, or when they reach the age at which their biologies have decided they should be raising kids. But these outliers tend to be the result of an intentional choice to remain open and seek out novelty. Without such efforts, we're more prone to refocusing on the stable and predictable as our biological clocks tick onward.

It's this predictability that is celebrated by politicians when they accuse their opponent of being a flip-flopper. This other guy can't even make up his mind about how he feels on an issue! He's clearly naive and immature. How can we take anything he says seriously?

It's a clever political tactic, to make one's opponent seem less fatherly or motherly. To make them seem less like a parent and more like a rebellious kid.

That rebelliousness, though, is a consequence of our drive to seek out newness when we're young. Not all of us do it in the same way, and again, we're all at different points on a vast spectrum, but in general we tend to be more open, and even enthusiastic, about new stuff when we're younger.

Unpredictable things are great, surprises are great, new people are great. Let's go over there, what's that, tell me why this works the way it does. We see amplified versions of this tendency in toddlers, as they don't yet have the social savvy to pretend they don't care about things. But we see it in teenagers and twenty-somethings, as well, it's just presented differently. Maybe we're attracted to the outsider kid in high school, not because we know much about them, but because they're different. Maybe we aggressively seek out new music, because knowing about what's new is a value proposition within our social clique.

Conflict emerges between older people and younger people as a result of this. Parents want to take care of their kids, ensuring they have stable ground to stand on, that they don't get into too much trouble, that they don't go exploring dark caves full of bears, that they don't date shady and maybe dangerous individuals. Kids, in turn, want to break free from parental limitations, absolutely dying to expose themselves to new things, new people, new ideas, new parts of town, new experiences, new everything all the time always.

The drive for novelty makes it more likely that, at the most reproduction-focused periods in our lives, we have a wide variety of options and a wide variety of metrics to use when choosing mates. This is the biological purpose of the penchant for newness in young people. The perceived "cool" of novelty or unfamiliarity is this reproductive drive filtered through our social lens.

But the rationale for this predisposition doesn't stop there. As social creatures, by exposing ourselves to more things, we become richer, deeper, more well-rounded individuals. This can make us more appealing mates in some cases, but it also makes us more likely to survive in a wider variety of contexts. Physiologically we're more hardened against disease due to our exposure to more germs and environments. Sociologically we're more capable of thriving under different sorts of governments and within different industries, and fitting in with different groups of friends.

As we get older, the challenge is finding a balance between these predispositions.

Yes, we're more likely to seek novelty as youngsters, and yes, we're more likely to prefer the secure and familiar as we get older, but none of this is destiny. These are tendencies sparked by biology and reinforced by social mores, but there are many things our biologies have instilled in us which we successfully ignore or suppress. There's no reason we can't derail these drives, and there's no reason we can't make them work for us, rather than against us.

Our taste buds die and regrow consistently during the first half of our lives. At around age 40, however, they stop regenerating. At around that same time, our olfactory senses start to dull. The result of this regression is that by age 80, most people cannot pass a taste or smell test: we lose our ability to sense things reliably.

Studies have shown that most perfumers, however, have olfactory senses that get better with age. They can smell more acutely and accurately at age 50 than at 30, and even more at 70 than at 50.

What makes the difference, it seems, is not just being exposed to smells their entire lives—we're all exposed to fragrances every day, and we don't all retain our sense of smell, much less improve upon it, later in life—but the intentional focus on differentiating between them. Brain scans used in the test indicate that the part of their brains responsible for noticing differences between aromas stayed open and clay-like, and consequently, the body continued to keep the requisite sensory organs refreshed and active.

What we can learn from this, and from other studies that have been done on other senses, and things like memory and academic accomplishment, is that by staying intellectually active and exploratory, we're able to keep our bodies and minds functioning at a much higher level, longer.

It's not enough to just smell the fragrances that drift our way every day. We have to take the time to pull those aromas apart, to figure out what components go into them, and compare and contrast them with others. We have to be awake and aware, not just alive. We have to be participatory in our own lives, and give our mental capacities a reason to keep operating and expanding, otherwise they will, quite understandably, if we're using biological logic, begin to shut down to save energy.

The questions we ask as young people, then, are just as valuable as we get older. How might we tap into our enthusiasms and pursue them? How might we retain the thrill of anticipation and unfamiliarity, rather than giving in to the knee-jerk "this is a threat, let's retreat to familiar ground," response? What's that over there? How's it work? Why?

Part of why this is often difficult, I think, is a matter of self-perception. Seeing ourselves as explorers, as citizen philosophers, as people dedicated to extracting as much joy and knowledge as possible from the world around us, can't help but orient us toward things that make us happy. Exploration and regular exposure to the unknown doesn't just surprise us, it allows us to derive more value even from the evenings we spend at home alone, reading a familiar book and listening to familiar music; it keeps our minds primed to seek and learn and acquire information even in well-known settings. We can dig deeper into the familiar, get more out of it, if we're biologically and mentally primed to explore. To pay attention. To pick it apart and figure it out.

Discomfort also plays a role in our difficulty in dealing with novelty, I think.

Being able to cope with intellectual discomfort—to face cognitive dissonance and take in new ideas, to consider and assess them, to compare them to ideas we already accept and which may need replacing, and then to do so, if warranted—allows us to keep growing, and to become stronger, rounder, and more resilient with each new bit of information we acquire.

New information that contradicts our existing ideologies is not a threat, it's an opportunity. It's a chance to correct misinformation that colors our perception. It's a chance to start exploring a completely new corner of human experience. Seeing things in this way, seeing the unfamiliar as a positive, rather than a negative, ensures we continue to explore the world intentionally, taking more in, keeping our minds and bodies active and open, and consequently, fully experiencing whatever it is we're most passionate about.

Changing one's mind, according to current scientific understanding, actually requires more energy than holding down the fort and refusing to acknowledge anything that seems to disagree with our current perspective. Opening yourself up to the possibility that you're wrong, or not completely right, requires willpower, and willpower uses up glucose, which is what powers our brains. When you become short on glucose, you also become short on willpower, hence the exhaustion you might experience after a massive expenditure of willpower, or the lack of willpower you might possess after completing a mentally exhausting task.

Retreating to the familiar, then, and opting for security over accuracy, is the lazy way of doing things. Yes, it's more comfortable, because you needn't ever wonder whether you're living in accordance with a long-held mistruth, or if you've been making decisions based on bad information or improperly aligned ideals. You needn't expend all that glucose, and exert all that willpower.

But the effort is worth it. The melding of exploration and security isn't easy, and at times these two desires will come into direct conflict with each other. But finding a balance is the only sure way to enjoy the increased stability and intellectual confidence of growing older, while also keeping yourself malleable enough, and intellectually awake enough, to remain yourself—a continuously evolving version of yourself—while doing so.

There's no reason you cannot maintain growth from the beginning to the end of your life. There's also nothing wrong with opting for increased predictability and security, if that's what you really want.

But it's comforting to know that we have the option to set our own paths, should we choose to do so.

Credibility

We are irrational, we all have access to different information, and we tend to give more weight to data that reinforces our preexisting opinions about how the world works.

It's no wonder, then, that the modern world is experiencing a credibility crisis.

Even if we want to pierce our information bubbles, and even if we want to seek out higher-quality information, how will we know we've found it? How can we compare sources of information when they all look and sound alike? How can we know we've found a news source that's informative, rather than slanted? How can we know we're being fed a healthy diet of balanced information, rather than propaganda that claims balance because in doing so, it convinces us to thoughtlessly consume more of it?

I spend a great deal of my time and energy consuming and parsing news and other sources of information. And I feel, most of the time, that I've managed to find a good balance of resources, each of them cancelling out some of the weaknesses found in the others, resulting in a reliable whole.

But I still can't help but wonder: do I think this because of my own information bubble? Are my prejudices creeping through, making me think I've found something reliable, when in fact I'm merely convincing myself I have because I'm getting biased information that aligns with my existing biases? When I encounter someone who has come to wildly different conclusions than I have, and who gets their info from a different array of sources from mine, are they wrong or am I? Which of us is deluding ourselves into thinking we've found balance? I'm inclined to think that I have found the truth, but they are no doubt inclined to think the same about themselves.

I think it's likely there are aliens out there in space. It seems incredibly unlikely to me, in fact, that there are not. The question of whether they've visited Earth is far less certain, but I don't think it's impossible. Now, knowing that I think aliens are probably real and their having visited us isn't impossible, I require more proof than other people might when it comes to claims of aliens on Earth. I want to believe it, and as such, I make sure to counter my bias by demanding far more evidence than people who are natural alien non-believers.

This approach tends to result in more balance and less bias in one's news, but it's also difficult to manage because we're often unaware of our own biases, until and unless others point them out to us. And when this happens, if it happens, it's more likely we'll become defensive, denying what seems to be an insult or accusation, and reinforcing our internal arguments: reminding ourselves of how clever we are and how informed our perspective is. We might then downplay the opinion of the brave soul who challenged us, giving their words less weight. This same predilection is seen in how we consume news and hear opinions that contrast with our own: if they don't make us feel smart and like we have all the answers, we're inclined to subconsciously tune them out.

Which, of course, reinforces the bubble in which we live.

This predisposition is what social networks have tapped into, building algorithms that make us feel smart and which reinforce our existing biases rather than challenging them. How many people would log in to Facebook several times a day if the majority of what we saw weren't articles and videos that love what we love and hate what we hate, but rather the opposite? How often would we return to a social network that presents us with nothing but well-informed, well-reasoned arguments about why we're probably not as smart and informed as we thought? What if these networks asked us to consider the superiority of another governmental system, another religion, or another brand of smartphone? What if, instead of being fed a steady stream of feel good messages or outrage-inducing clickbait, we were intellectually engaged and rationally confronted every time we logged on?

We probably wouldn't log on very much. Or we'd change networks, refocusing our attention and clicks on the competitor that gives us the fun stuff, the "good" stuff. Because in this context, "good" isn't educational or informative. It's relaxing. It tickles the right emotions, rather than making us feel uncomfortable, the way that new information from outside our existing bubble makes us feel.

When we expose ourselves to new ideas, particularly those which might challenge how we act and how we come to conclusions, we're also forced to take responsibility for these actions, these biases. If we've spent our lives hating, or at least feeling superior to a particular group of people, but then are exposed to convincing information about that group that makes us hate them less, that's a very awkward moment. Taking this new information seriously would mean having to choose between continuing on as we are now with our existing biases, our existing way of interacting with these people, our existing group of friends who probably have the same set of biases that we now feel compelled to question, or changing all that. Maybe losing those friends, maybe forcing ourselves to awkwardly face this group that we've treated so badly on more equal terms.

Mea culpas aren't easy or pleasant. They aren't for the faint of heart. And it's not that we're all too weak to make such changes, it's that we've seldom had reason to. We're all so capable of bunkering up, our biases and brilliance constantly reinforced, that to be offered an alternative that makes us feel less informed, less smart, less good and noble, means the choice for many of us is clear. Why put ourselves through that?

The credibility crisis is not just the consequence of fake news and new technologies seamlessly blending rumor with fact. It's an internal crisis we all face, and one we're compellingly incentivized to ignore. Combine this with those other issues, and we are suddenly unable to easily distinguish fact from fiction, propaganda from well-balanced reporting.

Within the United States, one of the most well-known and visible efforts to influence a large chunk of the population is seen in *FOX News*. This was a network that became a huge success in a short period of time by mixing its editorial content with its real, fact-based news content.

This network has become, for all intents and purposes, the propaganda wing of the Republican Party. This is not a value judgment: the move was brilliant and savvy. It showed an understanding of how things were and where they would go next. The history of journalism is steeped in slanted reporting, and the fact that *FOX News* managed to revive that tradition within the United States, and do it more successfully than any historical example, isn't inherently negative. What happened as a consequence of their success, however, led to an arms race between the networks. And the rhetoric slung by *FOX News* and their progressive competitors resulted in a growing gulf between Democrats and Republicans. The US became far more polarized than it already was.

That *FOX News* calls itself "fair and balanced" is itself a joke to anyone not deeply entrenched in the conservative political bunker. You can agree with much of what they say and still agree that such a statement would be silly, if it wasn't so harmful to the concept of unbiased reporting. That brazenness, though, is what inspired other, opposing networks to bloom, and even led to the birth of further-Right networks, which used the same tactics as *FOX*, but in support of far more extreme ideological positions.

The *Huffington Post*, I would argue, is the best liberal analogue for *FOX News* in the United States. It is just as likely to produce real news as *FOX News* is, but that news is presented alongside hard-edged editorial pieces that reconfirm the biases of its intended readership, and the language used within the news pieces gently bend the information, as well. When reporting on abortion, for instance, *FOX News* will use the highly misleading, but common-on-the-Right term "partial-birth abortion" to describe a specific abortion technique, while the *Huffington Post* will be more likely to focus its reporting on the rights of the mother. Both of these perspectives are correct, and even with the misleading labels, both can provide technically factual news. But the slant is evident and it's part of what has brought us to where we are today.

Where we stand now, news-wise, is an uncomfortably high, narrow, and slippery precipice. There's an immense amount of incredible, factual, rational reporting being done, but that reporting is often given second-billing to the more confrontational and biased pieces. This is in part because the latter are presented by the more economically successful and culturally popular networks and sites, and in part because, frankly, the more important work, in the sense of educating oneself with well-reported and supported information, is also often less sexy. The "if it bleeds, it leads" tendency of the press means that a vitally important bit of information may be available in the newspaper and on the internet, but it may also be completely ignored, overshadowed by a piece of gossip.

Fake news, the kind that is sucking the oxygen out of the room, anyway, leaving little for the legitimate reporting that's taking place, is not the "Bat Boy Lives!" style of "reporting" that has been featured on the covers of grocery store tabloids for decades. The fake news of today looks real, feels real, and might even contain 90% real information. That other 10%, however, is the poison in the chalice. It's immensely slanted information that often references another piece of false information we may have heard elsewhere, which was in turn planted for us to find to reinforce another story. Sometimes it all traces back to a blatant lie, but more often their mixture of truth and fiction tells a very specific story, and almost always the moral of that story is, "You can trust us and only us, everyone else is lying to you."

Think about that for a second.

If we're getting our news from slanted sources that tell us all other sources of news are lying to us, then we are closed off from any information that might help us establish complete context. It's as if, before we can take a good look at the world, we're convinced to wear blinders, and to attach them in such a way that they cannot easily be removed. We're locked into one particular system of information dissemination so that, even if what we're being told becomes obviously, laughably fictitious, we'd have no way of knowing. We have no source of comparison, because everyone else, we're told, is a liar, trying to play us for fools.

It's a problem that falsehoods are presented in the same way, with the same design, and with the same visual authority as real news on the internet.

Colin Wright

It's a problem that we don't trust journalistic institutions anymore, in part because of their failings, and in part because we're told not to by groups and publications that don't want us to have a means of checking their math.

It's a problem that we have political figures from all political parties telling lies about the press, because the press is our only means of holding these figures accountable. A powerful politician unchecked by a trusted journalistic entity can get away with murder while leaving the public none the wiser.

It's a problem that we've been primed to expect quick-twitch bits of information by our gadgets and communities, which in turn keeps us from being exposed to complete stories that help us see and understand the complete context.

It's a problem that the economic system which underpins the journalism world is predicated on advertisements and billionaires, the latter implying a powerful person's interests guide some of what's published, the former reinforcing the industry's fixation on clicks and page views over well-presented information.

Our perception of credibility is crippled, and there's no easy solution to this problem.

An awareness of the problem helps, because it allows us to counter our own bias, and to take everything we hear with a grain of salt and seek out more sources and counter-arguments for stories that seem a little too convenient. When we hear nothing but what we want to hear—our enemies are horrible, our prejudices are clearly right, our people are righteous and good—we should question those narratives.

Even if we don't change our opinions, we might be capable of changing the scope of our perspectives. If we do, our opinions will be much better informed, the connections between things far more clear, and the world made up of more grays, instead of just black and white.

Labels

Labels are reductive. This is part of what makes them valuable, but it can also make them treacherous if used too casually.

There's a discussion method I like to use when I'm having a conversation with someone with whom I disagree, but who seems to be open to sharing their thoughts and learning about my opposing viewpoints. The rules are that neither of us will aim to offend or assume offense is intended by the other, that we primarily ask questions and give answers, focusing on saying why we believe what we do rather than saying why we don't believe the opposite, and we avoid using labels. If we do use labels at any point, they have to be thoroughly defined.

The first few rules probably make sense to anyone who's been in a throw-down discussion that's taken a turn for the worse. We tend to assume that the best possible result of such a conversation is "winning" in the sense that we make better points than the other person, or failing that, we counter their points, or even attack their character, rendering their points moot. We may also infer offense when no offense was meant, which in turn allows us to feel justified in using our own verbal weaponry, sparking a standoff or shootout even when both sides would have preferred to keep things civil.

It's also easier to have a valuable discussion when, rather than making statements about what we believe the other person believes, we instead ask them questions about their beliefs. Instead of predefining them and their ideologies, we ask them to explain both from their own perspective. This incentivizes exploration rather than accusation, and allows us to expose our ignorance without feeling like it will be used against us.

Avoiding labels, though, can be a less clear proposition. What are labels if not shorthand for a collection of ideas and complex properties? Isn't that useful in getting to the meat of a discussion?

The troubling thing about labels is that we very seldom have the exact same definitions for them. If I'm engaged in a discussion about politics and someone uses the word "Republican," there's a good chance the other person's idea of what that label represents will be different from my interpretation of it. The same is true of "Atheist" and "African" and "Artist" and any other label we might choose to apply. There might be common attributes we would apply to people who wear these labels, but the differences in specifics are what derail us.

The result of using such shorthand is that we talk past one another. We cannot understand how the other person comes to such wildly different sums, when in fact we're working from completely different variables even before any formula is applied. It's no wonder, then, that these discussions can result in confused feelings and frustration: we're not even talking about the same ideas and people and beliefs.

This is why it's worth taking the time to fully explain the labels we use, or to leave them out of the conversation completely. This isn't easy to do, and as soon as you decide to watch for them, you realize just how many labels we use in every discussion, even beyond the exploratory ones. But it's worth the effort if you really want to learn, understand, and communicate clearly.

Labels have the potential to elucidate, not just obfuscate. If I tell you that something is dangerous, that it is a Dangerous Thing, you have been given very concise and useful information that might keep you from harm. That's evolutionarily useful because if we can quickly summarize gobs of information under one unified header, we can share more information in less time. The bandwidth limitations of language are bypassed, in the same way that compressing files helps speed up data transfer on a computer network.

But like compressing an image file, such a process can lower the quality of what's being compressed. There might be artifacts or a loss of color fidelity. When you compress a JPEG image file, one way the computer can reduce the file size is by taking each block of nine pixels and flattening it: instead of nine different colors, you now have nine pixels of a single color. This generally isn't visible when done to, say, a photograph, because most modern photography has so many pixels that the rounding-off and averaging isn't visible when looking at the photograph at its full size. It's only when you zoom in that you realize the image has been simplified, the pixels more boxy and large, the complexity of the image lost.

This is what happens with labels, as well. On the whole, when we're looking at the big picture, we don't notice the loss in complexity. It's only when we zoom in and take a closer look that we realize just how much clarity and detail we've given up for the benefit of faster transmission.

It behooves us, then, to avoid compression when having detailed discussions. It's offensive when someone lumps you in with other people whose ideas are similar to yours in some ways, but really quite different from your own on the whole, because it implies that they don't find those differences to be compelling, though they are quite important to you.

The only way to avoid these accidental offenses completely is to avoid labels. But because of the aforementioned benefits, we're biologically wired to prefer them, and their practicality often outweighs their detail-dulling downsides.

What we typically call "instinct" is a collection of subconscious triggers and actions that allow us to respond to something before our conscious minds have fully registered all the data and come to conclusions based on that incomplete assessment. That means we can encounter something new and not understand why it makes us uncomfortable; our subconscious has already pulled in a bunch of data that we haven't consciously acknowledged, and has come to a knee-jerk conclusion about this unfamiliar thing.

This is fortunate in that it allowed our ancestors to quickly get the hell away from predators, even if they'd never encountered a particular species before. It also means we're able to quickly read other environmental signals—this tastes sweet, so it probably contains plenty of life-sustaining calories, this tastes bitter so it may be poisonous to me—and we're more likely to survive as a result. Humans who are wired to trust their gut have, throughout history, had a better chance of surviving and procreating and passing on their genetic information to the next generation. There's a vast spectrum for this, as with anything, but a predisposition toward instinctual information gathering runs deep in the human species. We're all descendants of instinct-trusting survivalists.

The benefits of instincts come with downsides, unfortunately. Prejudice and bias stem from this same set of ancestral tools, because our past experiences or collected knowledge inform those knee-jerk reactions that we experience in the future; they make up the lens through which all this information is filtered.

If I've been told all people of a certain ethnic group are

bad, when I encounter one alone on a vacant side-street, I'll be far more likely to experience discomfort and fear and mistrust than to be open and assume civility, the way I might with someone from my own perceived tribe. In this way, racism and classism and prejudice against those from other faiths or belief systems can be transmitted from generation to generation, and from person to person. Instincts are not magical or supernatural, they're informed by the data gathered from our environment. And part of that data is what we take in from our parents, family, friends, leaders, and culture.

On the societal scale, labels are often used to delineate between Us and Them. This helps leaders explain why you are part of this group, and why that group is bad, why their ideas are not as good as our ideas, or why their lineage is not as good as our lineage. Leaders who amplify these divisions increase their own power, as it provides them with a bogeyman to scare dissenters and help keep the peace. It allows them to show why they are correct, why they are chosen; look at this other group doing different things, look how bad they are and how good we are! It's easier to celebrate one's own methods and beliefs if you compare them to an outsider's methods and beliefs. It's trickier to feel like a tight-knit group without an Other to look down upon.

Remember that the differences and similarities we choose to focus on when applying these labels are subjective, and suit the needs, or perceived needs, of the leader instilling or reinforcing them. If you decide that skin color is important, and you divide into groups based on that difference, you've decided that attribute above all others is important. That most people have five fingers, walk on two legs and two feet, have a pair of eyes, have hair, eat food to survive: that's all ignored. That we have far more in common than we have differences is ignored. We choose to fixate on differences

Colin Wright

because it serves the purpose of having an Other to look down upon. It allows us to identify ourselves as a group in contrast to them, rather than relying on our own traits, our own beliefs and individuality, to do so. Their shape, in a way, determines ours.

We choose what is significant and insignificant in this regard. We decide to imbue significance in skin color, or religion, or whatever else. We decide that where they were born is significant, and then seek out information to justify this bias.

It's a powerful thing, this realization. Because it means, since we are choosing what's significant anyway, we can choose to think of the things that divide us as insignificant and place increased significance on our similarities.

If we chose to, we could reduce the importance of the labels that divide us, and focus on those that pull us together.

We would be far better off if we were to bridge gulfs between cultures, even if this didn't mean those groups would become best friends or consider each other family. The ability to communicate between communities is a strength because it allows us to cross-pollinate and share ideas, perspectives, and even genetic material. This diversity strengthens the species, and makes all of us more varied and resilient, rather than "pure" and frail. A group separated from all other groups might be mighty in the one or two traits that they consider to be most significant, but having the best skin tone according to their standards will have come with its own downsides. Mixing and melding with the tribe across the way, however, allows them to share some of what they've long considered to be vital, while also reducing their own weaknesses; filling in the gaps that have emerged as a consequence of fixating so completely on just a few traits out of millions.

Labels, over time, evolve and mutate. They even lose their meaning sometimes, due to overuse.

I would argue that the term "Nazi" has lost a lot of its meaning in modern times. And this is unfortunate, because the label, derived from an actual group who did actual things and had actual beliefs, was a very quick, clear way of transmitting a collection of complex ideas to each other.

Today, however, this term has been weighed down with intellectual and social baggage. It's been overused, and as a result it often comically signals the end to a conversation. The tongue-in-cheek Godwin's Law states that any conversation that goes on long enough will eventually result in one side comparing the other side to Nazis or Hitler. This law was posited based on observations made in online discussion forums, as it seemed that any disagreement, no matter how mundane, almost always resulted in Nazi comparisons over a long enough timeline. The consequence of this disposition toward hyperbolic comparison was the killing of the term "Nazi" as a useful, meaningful label. It no longer means what it once meant.

It could be argued that the same is true for many other political labels, like Democrat and Republican, or even Liberal and Conservative. It's gotten so bad that, in some cases, efforts have been made to move away from the now-tainted labels toward something as-of-yet unburdened. Liberals in the US, for instance, have rebranded themselves as Progressives over the past few years—a term they believe is less tainted by cultural baggage.

Labels are reductive. They are useful at times, and very appealing to those who want to communicate data to each other quickly, but they're still reductive. They reduce the precision of the information we receive in favor of concision. Labels allow us to lump people and groups and things together, which allows us to feel we understand these things, even when that's not the case.

Used intentionally, labels can still be valuable. They help us achieve a broad-strokes understanding of complex things, and provide us with the means to quickly assess a situation that might otherwise require immense study. But used unintentionally, labels add fuel to the fire of prejudice, reinforce our existing biases, and allow us to feel wise when we're more misinformed than ever.

Like any tool, labels are best used in moderation, with skill, and with full knowledge of their power and implication. They shouldn't be completely avoided, but they should absolutely be used with care.

Goals

If I work from home, but decide I'm going to get up early each morning, get dressed as if I'm commuting to an office, and then sit for a set period of time and work without distraction, what is it that I'm trying to accomplish?

The superficial supposition would be that I'm trying to replicate working at an office. After all, I'm getting up early, I'm putting on normal clothes rather than lounging around in sweat pants all day, and I'm getting to work immediately, rather than watching Netflix or hosting a brunch.

More consideration, though, might reveal that my actual intention is to ensure that work gets done and discipline doesn't dissipate, despite my having the opportunity to work whenever I like, however I like. I could, in theory, wear whatever I like, but I'm choosing to put on a sort of uniform which makes me feel like I'm getting suited up for a particular task. I could change my schedule or opt for no schedule at all, but that would also mean I'd be less certain to get done what I need to get done, much less in a reasonable amount of time.

Supposing this is the case, let's go one step further. If my goal is to maintain productivity within a looser, more liberated lifestyle, is this the optimal way to achieve that goal?

Said another way: is replicating an existing structure in a new space the best way to utilize that space?

Many famous Greek landmarks look the way they do as a consequence of their interactions with the Egyptians. Exposure to the massive stone constructions of Imhotep made Greek architects want to try their hand at the same. As a result, they began to rebuild many of their temples, including huge, famous works like the Parthenon, from stone, where previously they had been wood. Because they were simply replacing existing pieces with carvings from a new material, however, the new stonework often didn't make much sense, structurally. This somewhat accidental stone-that-looks-like-wood style is called "petrification," because it appears as if woodcarvings have simply become petrified, rather than the Greeks having fully committed to the new building material.

Wood and stone, of course, are radically different substances, requiring very different techniques to work with and build from. They can hold different amounts of weight, and they must be treated in different ways if they're going to resist the elements. The result of this moment in time in Greek history, which was quite productive, and therefore prolific, is that a large number of quite beautiful Greek stone buildings don't make sense architecturally. Many of these buildings are so completely unbalanced, structurally, that they're more art than design: they're beautiful to look at, but nonsensical as buildings.

The question of what we're actually trying to accomplish with our actions is important because it demands we question our existing habits, biases, and goals.

There's a sociological term that's relevant here: the Matthew Effect. This is also sometimes called "cumulative advantage." This concept says the rich get richer because they are rich, the poor get poorer because they are poor, the famous get more famous because they are famous, and bestselling books will sell increasingly more copies because they are bestsellers.

This concept is useful if you're an unscrupulous author who wants to manipulate sales data to get your book on the bestseller list. Figuring out how to manipulate that system, even if it requires a large upfront expenditure, could prove to be a good investment if it lands your book on a bestseller list.

But it's also useful when we look at the priority we give to certain actions and habits. The things that we've done for a while have a latent psychological advantage over things that we haven't done yet. They seem better to us because we've always done them, so we continue to do them. The rich get richer because they're rich, and the status quo remains the status quo because it's been our status quo.

If we can struggle past the Matthew Effect, though, we may find there are more options to choose from than we might have guessed.

If I look at what I'm trying to accomplish with my work-from-home morning habits, I might find that what I really want is to get my work done first, before anything else, each day. The specific pieces of my routine, then, aren't vital. They're merely components I've borrowed from past experience that seem to help get me into a productive mindset, and which keep me from neglecting my work.

Recognizing that this is the case liberates me to ask myself what else I might do to achieve this same end result. How might I achieve the same goal more effectively? More efficiently? How might I achieve it in a way that makes me happier?

Asking this is the equivalent of the Greeks asking themselves how they might build with stone and treat it as stone, rather than treating it like wood, which would allow them to develop wildly new structures and building techniques. Historically, it took some time before they got around to doing so, but when they did, the result was structures that were superior in almost every way.

On a personal scale, our goals are unlikely to require the invention of new architectural techniques. Instead, we can develop lifestyle experiments that result in a slow but certain evolution of whatever it is we hope to improve.

What defines an experiment from simply changing stuff around, willy-nilly, is a degree of power over the variables being tweaked, control groups to which you can compare the results of those changes, and a set period of time in which to test the different ways of doing things. The results are assessed after each experimental period, and from there you can decide which changes to adopt, which you'll gladly leave behind, and which you'll continue adjusting, trying new things until something clicks into place.

In the case of adjusting my morning routine, this might mean instead of dressing for work each day, perhaps I only do so four times a week, leaving the other three days as "sweat pants and t-shirt" days. Or maybe a five and two split would be better, or six and one. I could try working at night instead of in the morning, or moving my productive hours to the afternoon, immediately post-lunch. I could scatter my work hours throughout the day, doing one hour in the morning, another hour just after lunch, another before dinner, and one more right before going to sleep. I could integrate periods of meditation and relaxation into my schedule, setting aside ten minute periods before and after working to help assess how I might best spend the time allotted so my next round of productive hours will be even more productive.

I could do away with a rigid schedule completely, instead setting firm deadlines and allowing myself to achieve them however makes sense each week, based on other things I want to do with my time. Or I could cram a week's worth of productive hours into just two days, leaving the latter five days free to be spent on whatever the hell. I could use the time I free up to learn new skills, experiment with new hobbies, and maybe come up with other productive tasks that could evolve into a side-business. Or I could reduce my expenses so I have to do less work overall to earn a sustainable living, which would allow me to spend more of my time on activities and hobbies that will never earn me a cent, but which make me feel immensely happy and fulfilled.

There are no absolutely correct solutions to such a scenario, but there are solutions that grant me more of whatever it is I want out of life. I could instigate an extremely rigid routine that allows me to wring the most possible productive hours out of each day, and if that suits my mentality, and if it allows me to make the money I desire, achieve the prestige I crave, or to feel like my life is organized so I can finally mentally relax, that might be a optimal direction for my priorities. Likewise, reorienting my day so I have more free time to spend on things like reading books and drawing trees and hanging out with friends can also be a positive change in direction, if that's how I've been wanting to reshape my lifestyle.

One's goals should inform one's actions, not the other way around.

We're often told that this is how you should live your life, this is how you should spend your time, and this is the process to get from where you are to where all the good people are. This prefabricated ideology informs the goals we set for ourselves.

How many of us actually dream of being CEOs, with all the responsibilities and time and energy such a position requires? Some people, certainly. But for most of us, the idea of holding such a high position within a corporation is not a personally held dream, but rather the end-point of a series of steps we've been told to walk. We've been told such a position is an indication of success, and so we pursue it. It's a goal defined by our actions, and consequently not one that is fulfilling for many people who achieve it.

This concept scales up to the societal level, as well.

If we ask ourselves what we're really trying to accomplish as groups of people, I think we'll find a lot of the solutions we're working toward and have put into place are not, in fact, solutions at all. They're actions we take to get from one point to the next, but they probably won't help us get to where we want to be. We might be a little wealthier, or rather, some small group of people might be a little wealthier. We might have better roads, and we might have a stronger police force.

But what if we don't actually want more monetary wealth? What if what we really want is a higher quality of life, something that isn't always associated with money? What if having better roads just means more cars and more dependence on those cars, when what we really want is increased mobility and the freedom it allows, which could mean wider adoption of high-quality mass-transit options? What if a better police force just means more arrests, and more enforcement of inequitable laws, and the passing of more laws that result in more people being arrested for things that perhaps shouldn't be illegal to begin with? What if more policing means the need to have more measurable results, which, in practice, means more traffic stops and pat-downs, when what we really want is security, which could be achieved through other means?

We as individuals, and we as societies, have finite resources at our disposal. A limited amount of time, energy, money, and other resources. That means we have to be careful how we spend these things.

Setting up systems for growth is only a meaningful use of our time if that growth is attached to a metric that actually matters. Change for the sake of change is not valuable.

Change in the pursuit of goals that we intentionally hold, on the other hand, is immensely valuable, and worth the discomfort we might experience in pursuit of it.

And it is uncomfortable to go through periods of change. Upsetting one's morning routine can be devastating to one's emotional well-being and productivity. It can make one feel untethered and worthless. It can upset one's self-identity, strange as that sounds, because we measured ourselves in terms of how well we lived up to the standards we'd established. Losing faith in that system and its ability to get us where we want to be doesn't alleviate the pangs of remorse we feel for not living up to its tenets. Especially if we haven't yet established a new scale that helps us see how we measure up.

This is why it's important for us to understand not just where we're going, but why we're going there. Individually and society-wide, we need to know what we're working toward and the rationale for that effort, so we can make changes along the way, always making minor adjustments as we learn new things, about ourselves and about the world.

This approach makes the necessity for major shakeups less likely, but it also primes us to make dramatic changes, should they be required. It ensures we haven't attached our sense of self-worth to something that seems important but is not, like how early we wake up each morning, and whether or not we put on nice slacks before going to work. Those might be means to an end, but they are not, themselves, an end.

Pursuing what's meaningful is important, but just as important is understanding why we're pursuing what we're pursuing, and how we're undertaking that pursuit. Pay attention to the why behind your actions, and the how and what become a lot easier to define and control.

Responsibility

There are entire industries dedicated to making us feel small. They are monetarily motivated to keep us feeling unprepared, inconsequential, and incapable.

Many of the people working in these fields, for these companies, wouldn't define their work as such, and the official line they're fed, and that we're fed about them, is that the products and services they provide are the opposite, meant to help us grow bigger, feel stronger, be more competent and effective. But that's not the result of their work, and that's not the motive behind their business models.

The most obvious example of this effort can be seen in brands that attempt to sell us a lifestyle. In order to convince us to pay more for a product that can be had for less through another manufacturer, we must be convinced that this brand is associated with things we ourselves want to be associated with. So a car becomes not just a car, but a representation of our success. A handbag is not just a handbag, it shows that we have class and style. A phone is not just a phone: it represents our preference for the better things in life, and our ability to afford them.

The amount of money required by brands to keep this

system fueled is colossal. Consider that they needn't only pay for the initial brand collateral—the logos, the websites, the business cards, the packaging, the on-message words to be written across them all—but also the supporting advertisements and billboards, the partnerships with products and personalities who represent something similar to aspirational audiences, and the publicity events which associate a brand, a logo, and a product, with larger concepts, like "adventure" or "celebrity" or "creative."

Such efforts must be maintained in perpetuity. Apple is one of the most brand-stable businesses in the world: they've invested enough money and effort over the years that they don't really have to do much at all to get attention these days. And yet, they still spent $1.8 billion dollars in advertising alone, non-inclusive of other branding efforts, in 2015. That is not a wasted investment, of course. Apple's brand in that same year was estimated to be worth over $170 billion.

What does it mean to say that a brand is worth a certain amount of money?

These numbers are soft, in that they're backed up by the best comparisons and sales figures possible, but aren't exact dollar-for-dollar receipts. A brand being worth a certain amount is not an indication of how much money that company will earn from their brand in a given year, but rather the estimated value of the collective brand in terms of how much revenue it brings in as a result of its reputation, design, and other factors, as mentioned above. Apple has a very valuable brand because they've done an excellent job associating it with very favorable and sellable concepts, like "creativity" and "music" and "high-end" and "simple." If they started slapping their logo on any random thing and tried to sell it, that value would degrade over time. But they would make a killing for a while, as the purchasing public has come to associate their brand with a certain type of product and level of construction, and consequently will be more likely to buy something that falls under that brand umbrella based on those expectations.

People buy in this way because we come to trust brands as shorthand for certain qualities we look for in consumables. Apple isn't beloved by everyone, but you can bet anyone who doesn't like their products has some brand in mind that they do prefer, whether that means another large corporation like Samsung for their phones, or a less-flashy but well-respected operating system, like Linux.

This shortcutting works well because it's in these brands' best interest to offer consistency in their products. But that consistency is achieved through branding, and one aspect of successful branding is making consumers feel they need this widget, this gadget, or this service. And one of the best ways to do that is to make the consumer feel they are currently missing something. That they are not enough. That they are incomplete.

It's easy to miss this when you look around at advertisements and other marketing messages, because they generally seem fairly upbeat and positive. Unfortunately, there's almost always an undercurrent lurking just beneath that chipper veneer.

Perhaps an advertisement shows us how wonderful it is to be at a dance club, engaging with attractive people, dancing and smiling and laughing, going to the VIP section, having a dressed-up night to remember with good people. The message being conveyed is: don't you want to be loved by others? Don't you want to be perceived as attractive? Wouldn't it be nice to have a wild, carefree night, away from all the things you worry about all day long? All those things that stress you out? Wouldn't it be cool to be important enough, or wealthy enough, to be in the VIP section of a high-end club? And finally: this brand of vodka can give you those experiences, can make you feel that way, can make you that person.

No one in this ad is explicitly saying, "You're nothing without us." But that's the long and the short of it. It's a seemingly feel-good message with a deflating prologue. You are not who you want to be, let's see what we can do about that.

Much of the advertising we see every day follows this script, though set in wildly different environments and aimed at very different people. You're not being a good enough mother unless you use this specific butter spread. You're not really a man if you don't wear these jeans. You're not living up to your potential unless you go to this specific university.

Trace all the feel-goodism backward, and the foundation of these messages is universally and intentionally unsteady. You're meant to feel less-than. You're meant to feel like you're being offered a lifeline.

And this clearly works. All that money isn't being spent on a whim, or because the people running these companies think it might bear fruit. They know it does. The money spent on brand-building advertising is as close to a sure thing as you can get in business. As long as they use the right mediums, communicate their messages effectively, and reach their intended audience, they've got us.

We desire things, as a rule. It's biological.

The rare exception to this rule is when we manage to step back from desire for a while. When we can look around and say, "I've got what I need. I'm good." When we can put our wallets away and not think about how the computer we have back home sucks because a new model was just released, or that our torsos could use some trimming because the woman in the ad we just saw was skinny as hell and acting all casual about it.

These messages warp our realities. There are skinny people

out there, but that doesn't mean we are any less svelte because we've been shown an image of someone who's professionally thin. There are new gadgets on the market every day, but their existence does not change the utility of our existing machines.

The comparison is what gets us. Our computers seem like less because we're comparing them to this new thing that just hit the market. The same is true of how we feel about our bodies, how we feel about our positions in society, how we feel about our significant others and cars and social lives. We're made to feel like less in comparison to larger-than-life examples and strategically released novelty, because making us feel this way triggers our desires, compels us to catch up. To do better. To buy this thing that will make it all better. To spend whatever it takes to make ourselves better.

Even the ideologies we're sold, the ones that are supposed to make us feel good, make use of this tactic.

Diet books, self-help manuals, touchy-feely talk shows, they live or die based on how desperate they can make us feel to change something about ourselves.

The diet industry would collapse overnight if we all suddenly got very healthy, or felt fine the way we are. There's an economic incentive, then, to ensure we never get that way. This means they must either sell us things that won't get us to where we want to be, or forever ensure our confidence levels never get so high that we feel complete and worthwhile. Or both.

The same is true of the books about finding yourself and blogs about how to have it all. If you ever found yourself, you'd stop buying the books. If you ever had it all, you'd stop feeding them page-views.

There are exceptions to this out there, but they are few and far between. And even those exceptions are sometimes entwined with this model, not fully pulling their punches for fear of losing readers or viewers, but organizing their information in such a way that there's no end in sight. No mechanism through which the people on the other side of the transaction will ever be encouraged to go, do, live, be happy, and hopefully never come back, because that means they succeeded.

This unfortunate reality is a consequence of the version of capitalism that's been adopted globally, but it's also partially the result of our dismissal of personal responsibility. We might feel very rah-rah capable and confident much of the time, but that confidence and capability is often tethered to a service or product. How many of us would stop working out if our personal trainer disappeared or our SoulCycle location closed down? How many of us would know how to feed ourselves properly, sans the well-curated menu of that little vegan place down the street? How many of us would feel beautiful and socially comfortable and able to learn new things, lacking the encouragement of professionals, or the reassurances of coaches, mentors, and well-positioned gurus?

I'm not saying there's anything wrong with self-improvement. I'm very pro self-improvement, and pro health, and pro eating well, and pro living optimally, whatever that term means to you. But I am saying when we become overly reliant on outside influences, encouragement, and incentives in how we feel about ourselves, we open ourselves up to abuse and mistreatment. We open ourselves up to being manipulated.

In some cases this manipulation is well-intentioned. Government agencies which encourage us to eat more vegetables, for instance, might attempt to manipulate us into doing so by sharing data about how veggies are good for us, and recipes that demonstrate how we might integrate them into our existing eating habits. That, I would argue, is positive manipulation; a beneficent use of these tools.

Most uses, however, are not so altruistic, and even those with potentially positive consequences—like guilting us into getting a membership at that gym across town—may in fact keep us from considering other options that might be better for us and our individual needs. Maybe establishing a workout routine we can do at home would be more ideal for our lifestyle than paying for a gym membership we'll seldom use. Maybe there's a yoga place nearby which would provide a more suitable environment and type of exertion.

Filtering out these messages, and reinforcing ourselves so we aren't such pliant prey, is not easy. It requires we pay closer attention to what we're being told, and that we trace these messages backward to figure out why they're saying what they're saying, why they're saying it to us, what they're actually saying underneath the positive-sounding words, and how that message is attempting to manipulate us.

This sounds complex, but it's not. Much of what I've said on this topic is obvious to most people, we simply don't put in the time to intentionally call out what's being done, and work that data into the formulas we use to determine what we buy and whom we do business with.

What requires a lot more time and energy is bolstering your defenses against these sorts of messages. You can do this by ensuring you're not an easy target, which requires being confident in a way that is not dependent on outside reinforcement or approval. That means you understand why you do the things you do, and why you make the choices you make, including purchasing choices. It means you take responsibility for yourself and your actions.

Sometimes what's being presented really will be an excellent option for us and our unique needs and wants. Sometimes a particular brand really will consistently offer products with attributes we value, and which add value to our lives far beyond the monetary price paid.

But sometimes we're merely convinced they will, or that they do. There are a lot of smart people working tirelessly and spending billions of dollars to make us feel this way. It's no wonder it's an approach that's proved so successful.

Taking responsibility for our own needs means taking the time to figure out who we really are, what we really want, and how we might get there. It means deciding if that handbag really will be a valuable addition to our wardrobe, and if so, what we'll be giving up to get it. It means accepting blame for the bad choices we make, be they choices about purchases, habits, diet, relationships, or how we feel. It also means taking responsibility for the good choices, not owing everything to a particular diet plan or workout routine, to a philosophy or brand that changed our lives, but to ourselves. For choosing carefully, taking what makes sense from all available offerings, and carefully curating lifestyles that will most fulfill us. We own our mistakes and failures, but we also own our successes and victories.

We're not encouraged to do this. We're socially incentivized to place responsibility elsewhere; on other people, on our significant other, on society, on the government, on our deity of choice. If it's always someone else's fault, then we, personally, are not doing anything wrong. We just need a new guru. Someone who will take responsibility and tell us how to be.

This makes coping with failure and difficulty easier, in a way, because it foists blame on anyone but us. But it also belittles us, coddles us, and causes us to feel incapable of doing things ourselves.

It's a journey, not a destination, this process of bulwarking our self-perception against outside intrusion. We have to continuously stoke our inner flames of self-reliance and perceived capability.

Many of us spend our entire lives never starting along that

path, and instead fall back on old habits and pleasantly simple-seeming alternatives in the form of gift-wrapped self-help book solutions and brand-pushed purchases we hope will make us feel better, this time.

Choosing to take responsibility is lifestyle-defining. It affects everything we do.

Choose wisely.

Awareness

Our instincts are informed by our knowledge and experiences. This means they're flawed, but it also means they're trainable.

Which is to say the more we learn, the more we know, the wider our range of personal experience, the more fine-tuned our intellectual reflexes, our instincts, will become.

If I showed you a poster, designed and illustrated to attract attendees for a conference in Seattle, chances are you would have some immediate, innate response to it. It will appeal to you, or not. It will make sense to you, or not. We all have aesthetic instincts, and while none of them are wrong, they're all different. Again, our tastes in these matters are informed by who we are, and all the things that make us unique. Our differing opinions don't imply one person's taste is superior to another's, just that they have senses of aesthetics that are defined by different things.

That said, if you were to show the same poster to someone who has a background in design and illustration, they might be able to point out structural and aesthetic strengths and weaknesses of the piece. It makes good use of the rule of thirds, perhaps, but the typography is too condensed for a poster, and the contrast not high enough; the words won't be legible more than a few feet away. Further, while the graphics are beautiful, they don't tell you much about the conference or where it's being held, and the city skyline used in one of the graphic elements isn't from Seattle, it's from Portland.

Here we have a set of aesthetic instincts that have been sharpened by a completely different set of experiences and knowledge, and consequently, the designer sees things that the non-designer would have no reason to see. Someone who isn't educated in aesthetics or visual hierarchy would have no reason to consider that the graphic elements might be unintentionally displaying visual cues from another city, nor to wonder if the pertinent information is visible from a distance, as one might hope it would be on a poster. They'd also have no reason to assume that part of why they find the work beautiful is because of the division of the space into thirds, which is a composition technique based on the Golden Ratio, which replicates proportions found in nature and which humans tend to find beautiful. This last piece of ratio-related information is something we've been aware of as a species since the early 16th century, and yet most people are unlikely to think about it when viewing a design or piece of art.

And so, while one's taste is not directly comparable to another person's in the sense of "better" or "worse," you could absolutely ascribe a pragmatic value to the aesthetic instincts of a designer over those of a non-designer when it comes to, say, figuring out why a billboard isn't quite right, or how best to compose a photograph, or how a room might be optimally furnished and painted. The collection of information a designer has, and their experiences with similar situations in the past, make it far more likely their responses in such settings will be informed by actionable information rather than personal taste, the latter of which could be based on any number of things, many of them not relevant to the task at hand.

This isn't to say there's no way a non-trained aesthete would ever come up with design-related ideas that surpass those of a professional designer. There are people who have the visual equivalent of perfect pitch in that they latently understand spatial problems, like those related to proportion and composition, or can mentally blend and contrast colors in the same way a musician might blend sound. It's also possible an untrained person with no particular knack for design simply has a "eureka" moment, understanding for whatever reason what needs to be done to make a room feel more comfortable, or a painting more impactful.

This will be the result of their knowledge and experiences, but they likely won't know which combination of variables led to that particular idea. As a professional designer with over a decade of experience, I will sometimes construct or correct things based on knowledge of what tends to make for good composition and proportion, but in many cases I know what will work based on intuition, then circle back to figure out why it worked, afterward. The result will often be the same, because my instincts have been trained over the years, and my brain filled with knowledge on this particular subject, so my subconscious pulls up all that background and applies it without me having to consciously guide anything.

The same is true for auto mechanics who have spent years working on cars, and who suspect a particular component is causing problems in an unrelated area of the vehicle, even though they can't quite say why they think that's the case. This is also true of cops who have worked with people for a long time, and who have come to know when they're being lied to, or when someone is holding information back, even though they wouldn't be able to tell you if you asked how they know.

Training our instincts is like feeding our subconscious. It grants us more informed, helpful knee-jerk reactions, rather than blind and potentially damaging impulses.

I've spent the last six months learning how to cook, and though I'm still no chef, when you prepare all your meals for a decent amount of time, you begin to look at related things a little differently.

Going to the grocery store, for instance, is an entirely new experience for me now that I cook. Previously, I paid attention to different aisles, primarily those containing frozen foods and prepared meals. Today, I spend a lot more time in the aisles which didn't hold any particular appeal for me before: those containing ingredients, things that aren't food yet but which can be made into all kinds of things with the right knowledge and application. Flour and baking powder and salt and sugar and racks full of spices would not have been very valuable in the hands of the person I was six months ago. Today, though, these ingredients have unlimited potential.

As we learn more, we become more aware of the world around us. The grocery store is a far more complex place to me, now, because the percentage of the building that contains relevant products has increased tenfold. I now have reason to pay attention to all those bags full of whatever, because I understand how they fit together with all the other bags and boxes and sacks full of things.

The grocery store hasn't changed, I've changed. And in turn, the way I experience my environment has changed.

The same is true of any field or body of knowledge. There's a joke in the design world that if you really hate someone, teach them about typography. The rationale is that the world is so full of bad design, and particularly bad use of typography —on signage, t-shirts, billboards, the internet, everywhere— that you cannot help but see it everywhere you go. But you don't notice how bad it is, or know what rules are being ignored, until you understand the fundamentals of typography. As you learn more about design, you come to feel more comfortable when surrounded by beautifully designed things and uncomfortable around things that need to be tweaked or corrected. Badly designed signage you pass every day on the way to work can become torturous because you can see the flaws, almost viscerally feel the improper use of kerning, and that pain is a consequence of your typographic knowledge. Where once such signage may have simply blended into the background, now you know enough to see the flaws, and feel their dissonance.

Becoming more informed, more aware, has downsides. It means you're more conscious of the bad stuff: not just the terrible typography, but also the violence taking place overseas, the way children are abused by their parents all around the world, the mistreatment of people because of their religion or skin color or cultural heritage. An awareness of these things can be valuable, but it can also be painful. Just as learning to cook opens up all those previously uninteresting aisles at the grocery store, their contents once blurred by ignorance but now crystal clear and relevant, learning about history and conflict and politics and humanism and disease and economics and international relations can be both uplifting and soul-crushing. It can fill your world with more colors and shapes than you ever knew existed before, but in seeing these new elements, you also see all the negatives, the horrors, the corruption and sadness and pain.

You can't have one without the other. Increased awareness of anything increases your capacity to see and understand both bad and good.

Not many people would admit to keeping themselves ignorant for this reason, but many do. They don't intend to blind themselves to the good, but they do want to overlook the bad. They want to keep such concerns from infecting their conception of the world, and from tinting a perspective they can control and have come to understand. Additional complexity could weaken what they've built and the worldview with which they've grown comfortable. The tradeoffs, in their minds, are simply not worth the risk.

For some, intellectual blinders are a handicap enforced upon them by others: authoritarian governments, overbearing parents, societies or organizations that preemptively label anything they don't control as false or wrong.

For others, those blinders are self-applied. Which is a tragedy.

If all you've ever known is the color blue, different shades and tints of blue, and you've never seen any other color from the spectrum, it's understandable you might be skeptical that there are other colors out there, especially if attaining them requires some effort; perhaps you have to leave blue behind for a time so you can see red, so you can see yellow. Some people, perhaps most, would never leave their familiar, comfortable blue world behind, because the costs of knowing other colors might seem too high, too risky. What if they can't find blue again? What if perceiving new colors is a horrible experience? What if a multicolored world is more confusing and complicated than one that's mono-hued?

Once you see the other colors, you can't put your blue blinders back on. Not easily, anyway. The blues will still be there, but not with the same purity as before. You'll perceive blues mixed with all the other colors, inextricably connected, because there's nothing that isn't connected to countless other things, and as such there's no purity, no single-color perspectives in the real world.

Filtering is possible, but only at the expense of life's many connections and realities. You can live your whole life in a blue-tinted bubble, but only if you're willing to never see things as they really are. You'll see greenish-blue and never realize that it's actually yellow.

If we are going to pull off our blinders, we have to want to do so, and we have to be prepared for the consequences, both good and bad.

Is it possible to keep yourself and potentially your society sequestered from everything and everyone, and as a consequence to avoid much heartache and sadness, but also joy and fulfillment? Yes.

Is it advisable?

That's for each of us to decide for ourselves.

What We Don't Say

Daily, we make alterations to our shared hallucination of society. These transformations impact us, but also the physical environment upon which our society is built.

Among these changes are the increased and increasing shifts in our climate, and those structures intermingled with the climate and reliant on its stability. The oceanic food web, for instance, is an incredibly fragile and intricate pattern, predicated on the right balance of temperature, acidity, clarity, tidal patterns, and the reproduction rate of millions of different creatures, huge and miniscule. There's some give to its knit, but tug too hard on any of these threads and the whole convoluted ecosystem unravels.

The phytoplankton, which collect sunlight and convert it to energy, are eaten by zooplankton, which are eaten by small fish, which are eaten by larger creatures, which are themselves eaten by even larger ones, and this chain continues all the way up to apex predators, like sharks and dolphins and giant squid. Adjust the average temperature of the water a few degrees, or increase the acidity of the ocean a tiny bit, or change the flow of the currents so some areas become overpopulated and others become phytoplankton ghost towns, and all the predators that depend on these tiny creatures, directly or indirectly, disappear.

When this situation is explained to the public by the scientists who are watching it happen in real-time, the need for a change in how we conduct ourselves is emphasized. Less pollution so the climate doesn't shift so quickly. Less waste so the runoff doesn't end up in the oceans. More conscientious fishing regulations so we don't wipe out a rung of the oceanic ladder, wreaking havoc on all those above and below it.

What we don't say when having this discussion about global climate change and maintaining the environment and not demolishing our natural resources is that it's likely too late. We don't focus on how this is something that's happening, not which could happen. We haven't yet heard our politicians make statements about the new normal, about how weather patterns will forever be more extreme, about how these disasters we've been seeing worldwide aren't going to go away, that things are actually, probably, only going to get worse for a while. Maybe a long while.

We haven't heard them say this, but it's true based on information gleaned and presented by experts. Those who deny it for political reasons have access to this information, yet if they declare that something needs to be done, they only say that we need to prevent what's already happened from happening. They're speaking as if from another time, in another place, where ecosystems aren't collapsing and once in a thousand year disasters aren't happening every week.

There's method to this madness, I think. For some leaders, there's a lack of motivation to deliver the bad news because they don't want to be responsible for the panic and uproar such an announcement would potentially spark.

But another possible rationale is that by declaring the battle over, by saying we've lost, it's already happening, we run the risk of ceasing all efforts to keep fighting, to keep struggling as mightily as possible. And though even our canniest moves and cleverest strikes can't undo what's been done, there's still a very compelling case to be made for not making things worse. We can learn to survive regular hurricanes of historic proportion, but we're less likely to survive if half the world's landmass drops below sea level. We can learn to reinvent agriculture for an age in which the average temperatures are two-degrees Celsius higher than today, but we're not likely to survive an ice-less Earth, a situation that happened before, long ago, and which wasn't kind to species like us.

So although we know certain things to be true, we understand our predicament, we can't speak as clearly about it as we might want to. Doing so, especially from the highest positions of authority, might result in a worse future than if we obfuscate that truth. We present mistruths in an attempt to prevent truly dystopian realities.

As someone who values truth, in my personal life and in the public sphere, this concept is more than a little disturbing to me. I value good journalism because it helps us understand what's happening, and presents facts and data which show us how the world functions, what's working and not working within our social systems, and how we might make those systems better. I value good science because it's a process that allows us to more clearly see the world around us, what role we play in that world, and how our world fits into the larger, mind-bogglingly complex and massive universe. That there might be a logical excuse to conceal the truth, or at the very least obscure it, bury it, or not talk about it, makes me feel a twinge of regret and discomfort. Surely this can't be the only way. Surely this can't be right.

Whether it's right, morally, is up for debate. Whether it's the best solution of many bad solutions is, I think, more clear.

Ask yourself this question: if there was an asteroid hurtling toward Earth, and there was nothing that could be done about it—it's absolutely going to hit the planet, and it's going to end all life on Earth when it does—would you want to know about it?

I think many people, perhaps quite wisely, would say no. What's the point? If there's legitimately nothing that can be done, and we're assuming for the sake of argument there isn't, what's the point of knowing? Is pursuing knowledge for its own sake worth the cost of spending your final moments, or perhaps your final days on Earth, alive, in existential agony?

Consider what might happen as a result of announcing to the world that, yes, we're all going to die, and yes, there's nothing we can do about it. No one will survive. Everything you know, everyone you love, will be gone. There would be mass panic. Rioting, looting, raping, pillaging. Minor infractions would seem ripe for settling, perhaps violently. To some, this would be an opportunity to take revenge, or take what they've always wanted, at any expense, with no possibility of consequence. No consequence worse than what's already coming from the sky, anyway.

Consider, then, the alternative. Those who know, some scientists, some politicians, they bear the weight of this knowledge alone. Rather than telling the world the end is nigh, they allow the rest of us to go on with our lives, and we, having no reason to suspect anything unusual is going on, are able to live out however long we have left in whatever manner we would have lived those days, anyway. For some, things will be just as bad as they've always been. For the majority, it will be just as mundane as usual. For some, it will be a joyous time, the best days of their lives because they don't know the end is coming. They experience something wonderful in the time that was preserved for them.

There's a chance, of course, an announcement of this kind would not result in chaos and mayhem, but rather a joining of hands and voices, a coming together like nothing we've ever seen before. It's not likely, but it would probably happen in some places around the planet. It's possible.

That possibility, though, would probably not be considered compelling enough to convince those in the know that the opposite, horrible consequences are worth risking. The people with the knowledge, then, will not say what they know, because in concealing that knowledge, they're more likely to create a better outcome for the vast majority of people.

This is similar, in a way, to thinkers who assure those under authoritarian rule that, although the situation sucks, it'll surely result in some amazing art.

Sure, this may be true. A lot of amazing work has been borne of nonstandard, or even horrific circumstances. Being crushed, or feeling constricted, by an oppressive government is certainly one way to ensure creatives feel their work matters. But it could be argued that saying so serves little purpose, and can almost be counter-productive. If this will happen anyway, mentioning it only serves to reinforce negative ideas—that there are possible positive consequences of authoritarian rule—rather than highlighting reasons why such governmental structures should be opposed vehemently. I understand the desire to paint a rosy picture and be optimistic, but it could be argued we'd all be better off without such a statement, allowing the reality to take hold if it will, but not trying to sugar-coat it as it happens.

On a much smaller, less world-ending scale, the decision to speak truth or not happens all the time. In the case of the aforementioned climate and our impact on it, we have, in fact, left an indelible mark and there's likely no coming back from that. Short of a major geo-engineering effort that would be just as likely to mess things up further as make things better, we're stuck with this new situation, this new collection of sub-optimal circumstances, and we're going to have to learn to live with that reality.

We'll learn to build stronger buildings, capable of surviving immense earthquakes and historic hurricanes. We'll invent increasingly clever methods of food production and distribution, and correct imbalances in our contemporary economic system. We'll come up with new governing mechanisms which allow us to move faster and make smarter choices during periods of continuous crisis, and we'll devise new methods of relocating and housing those who are forced to evacuate their homes, whether due to drought or resource wars or deadly new diseases.

And we'll talk about these things, about solutions. Because doing so bears fruit, and it allows us to focus on the problems we can solve and the facets of our world we can influence and actually change.

Those other things, though? The major problems for which we have no solutions? It's unlikely they'll be debated by presidential candidates or discussed by experts on the news any time soon. Not because we lack the mental fortitude to deal with these issues, and not even because the people who might want to share are afraid to do so. It's because we don't have the social capacity, the right societal norms to have these sorts of discussions. We don't have them yet, anyway.

I wonder if we might be able to change that. If there might be a way to better engage with each other and with the systems that hold up our complex interpersonal arrangements, so we could not just survive the sudden awareness of an incoming asteroid or the truth about our current climate reality, but discuss it rationally, come to terms with it. If, as a society, we might be able to grapple with the complex, existential issues that plague us and which currently lurk behind a lot of the words we speak and things we do, as of yet unaddressed.

There is no solution to many of these problems, and yet I still want there to be. It's difficult to imagine what a positive outcome, lacking concrete solutions, might even look like. What a silver bullet-less conversation might involve.

But we need discussion, we need to be able to adjust our social pressure valves and mention unmentionables. If we're going to face increasingly complex and convoluted issues, we'll need a shared language and set of cultural standards that allow us to communicate without becoming shamefaced, without being worried we'll make things worse by bringing up uncomfortable truths.

If we can accomplish this, we may become more capable of solving most problems early enough that they never reach the point of no return. That's the ideal, anyway. But being able to have a meaningful discussion without the possibility of solution, to have that mutual-respect for each other's intelligence, emotional stability, and capacity to understand, is a worthwhile pursuit unto itself. When we accomplish that, we'll cease to be just a milling crowd of unconnected individuals, and become something more.

Legacy

The past seems so badass sometimes.

The clothing, the facial hair, the sternness and stability. People knew how to treat each other back then, you know? And men were men, women were women, and everyone was able to do a good, honest day's labor and then return home for a wholesome supper. We worked with our hands, back then. The always-on worry and complexity hadn't yet torn us down and made us into mere shadows of who we once were.

This is a common refrain; I hear complaints of this kind bandied about all the time. The past is held up as a magical land, a Shangri-La where we once lived happily, but then we lost it. We were cast out from this glorious Eden, possibly as a consequence of rock and roll music or sex before marriage.

Even young, contemporary folks fall prey to this ideology, this predilection for the past. We reach backward and appropriate what we can, adopting their look, their handcrafted things, their unsmiling facial expressions while posing for photographs.

What we often fail to realize, though, is that the perceptions we have are inaccurate. In some cases our ideas about the past are merely incomplete, but in other cases they're outright mythologized and wildly misaligned with reality. Sometimes we recall only the pleasant, mild parts of the story, leaving out the bad stuff. These things we try to forget, and in some cases actually do succeed in forgetting, lead us to make the same mistakes all over again, this time by a younger generation that never saw firsthand the consequences of the actions of their forebears.

The clothing styles of the past were not the consequence of an aesthetic preference, but more often the result of economic and technological conditions beyond the control of the wearer. Thick, harsh fabrics and simple adornments, or no adornments at all, strike us as minimal and clean, honest and natural. But back then it was the result of low-grade industrial machinery able to produce no more than the simplest of textiles at a decent price. Most people owned one main set of clothes, and wore them every day, with perhaps a few, nicer items for holidays or religious ceremonies. Given the option, most of these people would gladly have thrown away their "good, honest" garb in favor of something more obtrusive and non-honest. But economic conditions for most people throughout most of history have not allowed them to indulge in fashionable finery. That we have so many clothing options available at reasonable prices, today, is an immense luxury, and one seldom appreciated by those who have never known anything else.

The wearing of facial hair by men has also often been more a matter of practicality than choice, as the cost of maintaining a clean-cut look, or the accouterment required to do so, was not always attainable by those of lower economic castes. There have been periods where the ultra-clean-cut look was more in vogue, and consequently if you wanted to get any kind of work and be taken seriously, you had to own and be proficient with a straight razor, using it daily or being fired from your job at the mill or hawking papers at the train station. But even that trend was a relatively recent thing. For much of history, men wore facial hair as a mark of age and status, specific styles varying between cultures, but in general the longer, more elaborate facial-coifs represented a heightened manliness. Again, that we have the option of going with or without, in most developed countries, says something about how far we've come, both in terms of technology, but also in diluting the overbearing patriarchal expectations of our forefathers.

Speaking of patriarchy: traditions of men being men and women being women almost always favor the former group over the latter. Men are in charge and make decisions, while women bear the children, make the food, and take care of the family. There's nothing at all wrong with this setup when two people enter into it by choice, both wanting those respective responsibilities, but in the past, there was no option. A woman holding a job would be a travesty. A man taking care of children, or cooking, or even marrying someone he considered to be a partner rather than a lesser-half, was unseemly and demeaning.

When we look backward in history and smile, longing for a simpler time, what we usually mean are the pleasant, wonderful things—both individual and cultural—that those times seem to represent.

When we think about traditional relationships, we're probably not thinking about how wonderful it was to be forced into roles that may not make sense for us or our significant others, but rather how much less intellectual angst was involved in determining how we'd spend our lives, and who we were. There were fewer acceptable options, so we walked the prescribed path. We followed the instruction manuals. It wouldn't have occurred to the majority of people to ever question that, at least not in any practical, actionable way. There were harsh social consequences for anyone who dared.

That we have the ability to question such things today, that we have so many options when it comes to what we wear, who we date, what gender norms, if any, we adopt, how we look, what kind of facial decorations we cultivate, and every other aspect of modern life, is remarkable. But it's also stressful. Understanding all these options is complex enough, already. But it's stressful knowing it's our responsibility to find the right combination of variables, for us as individuals. It's even more disconcerting feeling that if we don't, we may not be living up to our own standards; which are standards the modern world tells us we need to identify and pursue.

What's seemingly wrong with the modern world is the same thing that makes it so wonderful: the vast array of options we have available. Listen carefully to complaints about the world today, and you'll find this is almost always the case. It's not the world itself that's getting worse, it's our perception of it. Especially when compared to the relative simplicity of the past.

This is what happens in any field in which we've achieved a relatively high level of development. Agriculture allowed us to focus less on mere subsistence so not everyone needed to produce food in order for a group of people to survive. This allowed us to diversify our efforts and specialize. This also means we were able to focus more attention on things like warfare, but the majority of what we started to do with our time led us to become thinking, feeling human beings, capable of impressive undertakings, immense discoveries, and remarkable feats of creativity. If we had remained at mere subsistence levels, producing just enough to survive and nothing more, we wouldn't have liberated sufficient time to create art, to build structures, to experiment with social dynamics. We would have been too busy. We would have always been on the verge of starving to death, and resultantly any spare time or energy we had left over after harvesting food would have been spent trying to get just a little more extra food, in case we experienced bad weather or weevil infestations in the future.

The legacy our ancestors have left us, then, is an expansive range of capability and choice. And this is a true statement whether we're talking about our hunter-gatherer ancestors from tens of thousands of years ago, or our more recent ancestors from the World War II-era and early Electronics Age. Their standards and expectations were different from ours, but the way they lived, the sacrifices they made, and the things they created are why we have all these options, today.

Perhaps not surprisingly, it's often the older members of society who are most disturbed by the changes they see happening around them. They worked their entire lives to ensure their children and their grandchildren would have more options and opportunities than they did, would live in a better world than they did, but when those changes begin to happen and when those opportunities are taken, they can't believe it. They're caught off-guard.

When most of us imagine making improvements upon the world, we imagine them from our existing perspective, using our existing units of measurement. If you're an average Joe living in the US in the 1940s, a vast improvement on social norms might be fewer Communist sympathizers to worry about and more division between the races. There were certainly people who hoped for greater and more equitable integration between races and better-funded government programs that might be called, by some, "socialized healthcare," but it certainly wasn't common. That definition of better would not have occurred to many people, because they didn't know what they didn't know. They couldn't have imagined, being surrounded by the culture in which they grew up, and with incredibly limited access to information outside that bubble, that their grandchildren would have wildly different standards from theirs. And that many of the improvements they would live to see would, to them, not be recognizable as improvements, and might at times seem like the opposite.

This is not always the case, but it's common enough to have become a trope in fiction and song. Rebellious children adopt new, edgy clothing or music or habits, as the disapproving parents look on, unable to believe their kid would become one of the bad ones. They'll learn, the parent thinks. They'll come to see the world exactly as I do, and come to hold dear the same things I hold dear. Their standards will conform to mine.

Thankfully, that's generally not the case. In some instances, for some things, it absolutely is. There are aspects of life that are more prone to regressing to a previously held status quo than others. The persistence of traditional relationships, whatever that may mean in a given culture, for instance, is fairly remarkable. Even now, at a time in which marriage is less and less common among young people, even as those who get married are waiting longer and rebalancing the power dynamics within their relationships, the general expectation of such a bond is still standard. Yes, in many places around the world we have the freedom to explore different arrangements, or no arrangement at all, should we choose to opt-out. But this is still unusual. We haven't yet reached a point where polyamory or multiple-person marriages or dating for life but never getting married is the rule, rather than the exception. That moment may come, but not yet. This is an aspect of life that has proven to be quite resilient, even as other facets of society change around it.

Kids rebelling and eschewing the trappings of their parents is common, but it's also a sign that their parents have done a good job ensuring their children have more opportunities, options, and potentially fulfillment, than they did. If a generation of children falls into lockstep behind their parents and their kids then do the same behind them, that indicates several generations in a row have had consistency, but no growth. It represents a failure to improve upon anything because improvement and evolution necessitates change. It requires we reshape and break things. It means we have to shock the hell out of some old people because they gave us the capability, the right, the state of mind to do so; to do things that, by the standards of the past, would seem quite shocking.

Each new norm is the consequence of something that came before. Sometimes the people responsible for these gifts—those who serve as catalysts to causes, or who are the brains behind inventions—are well known and well documented in the history books. At other times, and far more commonly, they're just pieces of a larger whole: a collective of human beings which make up a loose, cultural demographic that has changed just enough from the demographic that came before them, and which has, itself, made some minor changes that won't be visible until seen through the lens of the next generation.

Some changes require a few generations to properly gestate and come to term. Others were planted long ago but were waiting on a particular moment in time, a particular individual, a particular new technology, to finally emerge. Others come into being so slowly we barely notice them even when they happen. The transition is so ponderous that the shift seems to have happened both long ago and to never have happened at all. In those cases, it's difficult to draw a line and say, "This is where everything changed," because only a fraction of a fraction of the change happened each year or each decade or each generation. Looking at changes in ourselves and in our societies, then, is a bit like trying to track the evolution of a tool that was invented multiple times in

155

multiple places around the world and which, as a result, seems to have always been a part of us, though we know that cannot literally be true.

When we think about legacy, we often think in terms of what's valuable and important today. We want to pass on our brilliant ideas, the things we've found to be useful and practical. We want our kids to appreciate the same things we do, because appreciating those things has worked out so well for us, and brought us so much joy.

It's a disconcerting thought that forcing these wonderful things on the next generation may, in fact, stifle our larger goal of ensuring they are better off than us. Maintaining stability and safeguarding against harm can unintentionally become the enforcement of rigidity. It's possible to hug a generation so tight that they never come into their own and have no room to grow.

We may succeed beyond our wildest dreams in raising a generation that is better off in every regard than ourselves, yet not recognize it when it happens. The danger is that we may, then, go in and try to undo the good work we've done. We may, in our inability to adjust our perspective in this matter, trip the kid we've taught to run fast, simply because they run in a direction which we never explored—or knock them down because they choose to fly instead of staying planted on the ground like a good, wholesome person. We'd do it out of love and concern, but that doesn't change the end result. This is doubly dangerous in societies where the older, more experienced members have more power than the young because they're able to change not just culture, but law, to suit their views and to manipulate their offspring. Disconcertion can become prohibition when those in power believe their long-held truths are more vital than those still gestating in the young over which they rule.

An awareness of this relationship and what it looks like

when it works won't necessarily help us avoid doing the same thing that essentially every generation before us has done. But it could allow us to join in on the fun.

If we're able to stay malleable and open to learning from our kids even as we teach them, we may find ourselves enjoying a future full of wise older people, their minds still open and liberated like when they were kids, working alongside younger generations who benefit from their presence. This serves the dual purpose of stimulating more cross-pollination between groups who see the world in different ways, and enhancing our societies' capacity to bypass the uncomfortable rigidity that seems to be so common when the experienced enforce their ideologies on those who are still experiencing.

Retreat

Sometimes there's no braver act than a retreat.

It completely depends on the circumstances, of course. There are moments when you're better off, in the long- or short-term, standing your ground and facing your fears, facing an enemy, facing an uncomfortable truth. There are moments when we want to retreat, but out of fear rather than rational assessment. The biological fight or flight mechanism produces a powerful chemical cocktail, and some of us are just wired to flee more than engage.

It's a good thing this is the case. If it weren't, there likely wouldn't be too many humans, if any, left. We've created cultural mythologies around great heroes who stood strong against implacable enemies, knowing that doing so would lead to their untimely demise. If the cause is great enough, I can understand the sentiment, but in some cases the things we choose to stand for are more petty than noble: braggadocio, pride, honor. These concepts mean more to some than others, but they're all concerns that revolve around feeling big, feeling worthwhile. They require we sacrifice ourselves, put ourselves in harm's way. This says something about our default emotional settings. If we're not confident enough to say, "Nope, not going to die because someone insulted my honor," we have to assume our cultural or personal outlook ascribes less value to life and more to appearances.

As I write this, in early 2017, a wave of political and ideological isolationism is blazing its way around the world. There's an ebb and flow to this sort of thing, and we tend to see waves of expansion and interconnectivity followed by nearly equal and opposite pulses of contraction and disconnection. I say "nearly equal" because the dominant human trend for the last ten thousand years has been increased interconnectivity. We're more entangled with each other than ever before, and though history has meandered in the particulars, we have little reason to believe the overall direction will change.

It's difficult to imagine what a true isolationist government or culture might look like today. The theory of isolationism is that by pulling back and not becoming entangled with other groups of people, we can focus on our own priorities and ourselves. We won't get caught up in foreign wars; we won't have to play politics on anyone else's terms. We can be our own people with our own priorities. We can move at our own pace and not feel compelled to change as other nations change. We needn't trend-chase or ever feel we've ceased to be a truly refined version of ourselves.

All of which sounds great on paper, but makes little sense in practice. Even before always-on, powerfully interconnecting technologies like the internet, governments that demanded isolation were soon opened up by others governments that wouldn't allow them to close up shop. The reason these outside forces were able to make this demand— as in the case of the US opening up isolationist Japan for trade in the 1850s, and Britain opening up inland China ten years before—was that they possessed far superior technological might, compared to the carapaced countries they were cracking open.

At different points in history, China and Japan were far superior, economically and technologically, to the European and European-offshoot countries which later threw them around like rag dolls. The reason for this shift in power? The immense, inward-facing conservatism of these formerly dominant powers.

I'm not using the term "conservative" in the political sense, but the philosophical. These cultures reached a height of prestige, wealth, knowledge, art, and commerce unseen in their respective bubbles of influence. But then, fearing change to the status quo, fearing their power may change hands, or that what made them great may give way to something new, something not as great, they sealed up those bubbles. They decided the risk inherent in change, in mutation, wasn't worth the potential benefits of evolution. To them, change of any kind was not positive. The only possible positive outcome was for everything to stay the same.

They managed to enforce this ideal for a long time. In China's case, if we measure from the Ming Dynasty (though you could arguably go back further), they managed to keep things more or less the same for nearly 500 years.

This is a difficult figure to imagine, coming from a young culture like that of the United States. My country isn't even half as old as that period, and the amount of change we've undergone since 1776 is immense. Yet somehow Chinese imperialism of roughly the same model managed to survive from around 220 BCE until shortly after the British attacked and forced them to interact with the world. There were several Golden Ages in those few thousand years, including the aforementioned Ming Dynasty period. But what do you suppose brought about these periods of wealth and prosperity?

Change. Mutation. Outside influence.

The Ming Dynasty was sparked by a peasant who revolted against his rulers, which brought new ideas and people into power, and eventually relocated the capital of China from Nanjing to Beijing. Prior to that, under the Tang Dynasty, which began in 618 BCE, the country flourished as a result of the wealth and the intellectual and commercial cosmopolitanism derived from the Silk Road.

There have been periods during which certain cultures have isolated themselves and thrived, largely unchanged and unmolested by the outside world. But these examples are limited to periods in which the outside world was also an unknown expanse. At the height of Rome, they believed the world ended at Portugal. It was easier to be isolationist back in the day, because something like a mountain range could, for the entire history of a culture, keep it separated from everyone else. They could be completely unaware, for thousands of years, that just on the other side of that uncrossable geographic barrier there exists another culture that believes completely different things, worships completely different gods, has completely different leaders, and speaks a completely different language.

It's understandable, then, why such early interactions between formerly divided people might have been so uncomfortable. Imagine coming from a culture that always held the same beliefs, only to meet another group of people with diametrically opposite beliefs. Their lack of belief, their lack of knowledge of your clearly superior ideas and language, are an insult. It shows that your belief system is just one of many, not the one, true language or the one, true religion.

Such meetings can't help but make you question things. Can't help but shake your faith. That, or pull inward, never questioning. Because screw all those ignorant savages out beyond the borders of civilization.

We face that sort of problem now. And again, this is not

new, but it is odd, considering the shape of the world we live in. Mountain ranges are no longer a significant barrier between people, because we can fly over them and see not just the mountain range, but entire continents, using satellite images available free of charge online.

Our awareness is so much vaster than anything the Ming Chinese could have imagined, and yet we still hold some of the same isolationist ideals they held, and for many of the same reasons.

No group ever decided to pull inward and cut off contact with the outside world because they believed their own group was inferior. Even the most isolated tribe living in the middle of the rainforest, fleeing from outsiders, has decided that something about their culture is superior compared to all those strangers out in the wider world, flying their iron birds and wearing their strange clothing. They need to remain removed from all that, so as to stay pure and untarnished.

There's an immense arrogance in this, and in that arrogance we find a refined version of what's called the Dunning-Kruger effect, which essentially says those who are low-ability or low-knowledge tend to overestimate their own level of ability or knowledge. When I'm learning a new skill, I don't know how much I don't know. As such, there's a good chance I will overestimate how much I know, because I've yet to learn enough to understand just how vast an undertaking I've started, and how low on the totem pole I am.

I picture learning new things as the pursuit of a horizon. You can see where you want to be, and you put in the work, the time, the energy, to try to reach that goal, to crest that mountain. After a great deal of effort, you someday reach it, only to find on the other side there are three new horizons in all directions.

Most people can relate to this with something in their lives, I'm guessing. Whether it's learning about math or art or automobile repair or sociology, we start out believing the horizon we can see is the only one, and once we reach it, we've achieved mastery. We get closer to that mountain range and assume we have achieved near-mastery, we're so close. It's only after pushing further, working harder, that we realize how mistaken we were. This process repeats itself over and over again as we reach each new horizon, only to discover a more complete scope of learning, and new set of horizons.

As I mentioned, it's often a feeling of superiority that causes us to pull inward, to separate ourselves from all those savages out there beyond our borders. If we were to learn more, of course, we'd find their culture is just as rich as ours. We'd discover that by combining what they've learned with what we've learned, we're all better off, with more ideas as to how we should live, how to entertain ourselves, how to cure disease and crest mountains. But to do so requires humility. It requires we accept we don't know everything, that we are not the best. It requires we accept others as peers rather than barbarians, and we acknowledge and expose our weaknesses, to ourselves and to others.

What we see when isolationist politics surge around the world is this same sense of pride and ignorance playing out in a slightly new way.

Today, we have unparalleled access to information that shows us how much we don't know. We can easily see that the world is full of peers, not barbarians. But for many reasons, we don't make use of these tools. Or we use them to blind ourselves to any data that might make us feel small, or weak, or susceptible to uncomfortable changes. These efforts are amplified by passive aspects of the platforms we use to communicate, like the social media algorithms that feed us steady streams of feel-good or outrage-inducing information at the expense of reliable facts and data.

We all have the right to be as isolated as we want to be. So long as we aren't forcing this ideal on anyone else, preventing them from exercising their right to live as they see fit, I don't think there's anything at all wrong with living like an ancient or sequestering yourself from people who are different from you. It limits your capabilities and growth potential, but that is also your right, if the tradeoff seems worthwhile to you and your priorities.

As nations, as societies, we have less of an excuse for embracing backward-facing escapism. Yes, we need to ensure we're taken care of at home. But the idea that we'll be better off if we cut ties with the larger international community is fallacious. The idea that isolating ourselves will help us keep things the same, keep things from changing, keep uncomfortable new realities from seeping into our lives, is laughable. It might momentarily slow access to and acceptance of novelty, but mostly we're limiting our ability to participate in the larger discussion.

When Britain opened up China, the isolated Chinese had change forced upon them by the far more capable and powerful British. The British had this advantage because they were expansive and connected to the rest of the international community. The Chinese were fragile and easy to defeat because they'd kept themselves separate, and as a result hadn't iterated and evolved at the same pace as the outside world. They maintained a sense of purity, yes, but at the expense of their strength and wellbeing.

What's true on scale is often true individually.

Sometimes retreating can be a good strategy because it allows us to assess the big picture from a place of relative safety. But to step away from a difficult situation completely and to leave it in the hands of others means we have no say in what happens next. It means we've given up on that relationship, or that professional challenge, or that global trade network. This doesn't mean these things will cease to exist, it just means we will not benefit from them, and we will slowly atrophy like unused muscles, while the rest of the world and all the people in it continue to grow. Just like muscles, cultures grow stronger when consistently stressed and challenged.

Burying our heads in the sand and telling ourselves that nothing's wrong and everything that's happening is someone else's fault is not just cowardly, it's ineffective. We need to make sure our own highways are maintained and schools are well-funded, but segregating ourselves from what is happening half a world away doesn't help us do that. It in fact hinders local efforts by making us poorer, less informed, and by limiting us to seeing the world from just one perspective, when more ideally we observe from many.

Retreat is only a viable option when it's temporary and intentional. There's nothing wrong with stepping back and reassessing one's strategy with the whole context in view. But there's something very wrong with assuming a lack of involvement means victory and shirking responsibility for what happens next is a symbol of strength.

Progress

We often associate progress with things like science and technology, human rights, and access to higher education. We also tend to assume that if we asked a denizen of the 14th century what they thought the next hundred years would bring, they would give us a cognizant prediction about improved knowledge, more rights for the serfs, and so on.

These associations and assumptions are flawed, as the concept of progress as something measurable and predictable —something almost destined to occur—is only about four hundred years old.

Step back in time to the beginning of the 17th century, and you'll find, in the East, the Ottomans, Persians, and Mughals growing in prestige and strength, the Japanese entering their isolationist Edo period, Russia suffering a famine that kills one-third of its population, and the Ming Dynasty on the brink of collapse. In the West, Louis the XIV rules over the Kingdom of France, the Inquisition is gleefully burning people at the stake, the Gaelic clan system is destroyed by the English after the Battle of Kinsale, and an assassination attempt against King James I of England, which later became known as the Gunpowder Treason Plot, fails.

Hidden amongst these events you'll also find a book, published by a man named Francis Bacon, quietly seeding an intellectual revolution. The book is entitled *The Advancement of Learning*, and it contains an observation that, by today's standards, seems utterly mundane. But by the standards of the early 17th century it was absolutely groundbreaking.

In this book, Bacon noted that throughout history, civilization seemed to advance as a result of observation and discovery, and a consequent change in operation and outlook. But before this could happen, new ideas would need to be converted into tangible reality.

It was not enough to understand a scientific concept, one had to transform it into practical technology. You could sit around and study electricity all day (which was something natural philosophers, the title held by scientists at the time, did in the 17th century), but civilization wouldn't change as a result of that discovery until it was made into technology, which allowed that knowledge to influence the real world.

We discover things through observation and thought. We experiment and learn how these things work. But it's not enough to simply know we can make steel: we have to put that knowledge into practice. We have to build a light bulb using electricity and advanced weaponry using steel.

Once we do this, we change things. The world shifts. History progresses and society evolves. We're no longer where we were, and there's a noticeable, measurable alteration in behavior.

I don't think many of us would have a problem with this assertion, today. A large percentage of the contemporary human population has a basic education and at least a superficial understanding of history. We also have many tools that allow us to record information, both personal and societal, so we can look back in time ten years and see how different it was from today. We can see how society has changed as a result of the development of the internet, of smartphones, of social networks. We can see and remember how we behaved and what we thought was cool and how we dressed and how we spoke, and being able to look backward and contrast all those things with their modern equivalents allows us to say, okay, yeah, it's absolutely clear these inventions have made a difference in how I live, even though I didn't notice most of these changes as they were happening, subtle as they were in the moment.

In Bacon's time, people had difficulty understanding this because most couldn't read and the pace of progress was slow compared to today. A lot was happening, certainly, but because of the limitations of the time period's tools, they were severely hindered in demonstrating and communicating which developments led to which changes. Life spans were also far shorter back then, so even life-long students of natural philosophy only had so many productive years to play with. Our global population was also far smaller, and a tiny percentage of the population was provided a basic education. It was unlikely any one person would survive long enough to think up grand conclusions even if they lucked into the right economic situation, the right education, the right mind, and the right governing system; one which would encourage their questions, rather than kill them for asking.

Yet, even in the science of progress, we see progress. Once these ideas were identified and written about by Bacon, thinkers of the age began asking themselves how they might utilize the concept of progress, and how they might become even more progressive, moving forward into the future, rather than falling backward into the dark, rusty past, as many intellectuals at the time imagined would be the case.

Bacon wrote another book shortly after *Advancement*, and in it he proposed a new alignment of the studies, separating natural philosophy from other realms of thought, and coming up with new divisions between science, the arts, and philosophy; an organizational system which would be largely recognizable to us today. He also decided that science was the most vital of the three, and though this is a debatable stance to take, it provided an intellectual foundation for the coming Industrial Revolution.

Today, we see progress as obvious and even predestined. We don't step backward into the past, we step forward into the future. That's how things work.

But historically, this has not always been the case. Forward movement in time hasn't always equated to evolution in technological sophistication. There have been periods, including the Early Middle Ages of Europe, after the fall of Rome, which are noted for their relative dearth of scientific development and art, especially literature, when compared to Roman accomplishments.

We've learned in recent years there actually was invention and art taking place during these supposedly dark times, often labeled the Dark Ages, if not on the scale and of the same flavor found in Rome at its peak. But this period, and others like it, still serve as examples of how progress doesn't always align perfectly with the movement of time. Though this in some ways depends on our definition of the word "progress."

Ask ten different people what progress means and chances are you'll get ten different answers. To many people, it means moving forward, improving upon what came before. To some, this refers strictly to the technological world, but to others, it's all about science, absent the physical manifestation of those discoveries. To yet others, it's moral progress that is most pressing, or perhaps it's a combination of all these things and more.

Progress in one facet of society can mean regression for others. Looking back at the Industrial Revolution, we saw immense progress in terms of technological sophistication, economic wealth, and things like communication and education. But we also saw a great deal of harm to the environment, to the underclasses of society, and to traditional foundations of power. This revolution, then, was progressive for those who valued the ability to produce, to invent, to learn, and to advance the embryonic forms of modern democratic republics, with power predicated on commercial exchange rather than holy decree or royal lineage. But it was a devastating blow for monarchs and for the Catholic Church. It was crippling for traditional artisans whose textile-producing efforts were replaced by the far cheaper, and more efficient and effective processes enabled by machines. Skilled labor was no longer the asset it once was, only a few years previous.

When progress comes to town, for every winner, there's a loser. The effects of these shifts, of this movement forward, will always have a counterbalance in the opposite direction. This isn't because it's destined to happen that way, and we've certainly attempted to reduce the negative effects of these changes in modern times. But because we live in an era of scarcity, and because we do have opposing ideas about ethics, about personal morality, about spirituality, about political ideologies, about humanist priorities, there still tend to be losers every time we welcome a new round of progress-related winners.

Sometimes, these losers are the result of a shift in power or wealth. Just as the monarchy began springing leaks as a result of the new capitalistic powerhouses that bloomed during the Industrial Revolution, many people working in professions that were valued before the widespread adoption of the internet have found themselves without marketable skills in this new, interconnected age. The same will be true if autonomous vehicles become the norm: truck drivers, of which there are nearly three million in the US alone, will have trouble finding work if software can suddenly do their job better, at a lower cost, and without ever needing to rest.

There's also often a shift in privilege, both economic and otherwise, that can leave people feeling like progress-related losers even when their situation is only changing relative to others, not in any absolute sense. Some political scholars have chalked up contemporary support for crypto-authoritarians in the early 21st century as the consequence of older, nationalistic people realizing that in an increasingly interconnected, globalized world, young people and immigrants and people who don't look like them suddenly have as many rights and privileges as they do. Lacking the advantages they've had over these other people their entire lives, they feel as if they've been demoted, when in reality everyone else has been promoted to a status closer to what these people always enjoyed. This is a misinterpretation of what's happening, but their feeling of demotion is still very real and we've seen some tangible consequences of it. In this way, people who enjoyed the benefits of other, earlier progress sometimes perceive the social progress that has made things like gay marriage legal as regression.

There is no field of study that is fully and completely partitioned from any other field of study. There is no human being who is completely isolated from all other humans on the planet, either. Even the most far-removed, island-living hermit experiences the consequences of anthropomorphic climate change and the microscopic bits of plastic and other trash in the water that separates her from physical contact with the rest of her species. There are no clean lines between philosophy and natural philosophy any more than there are clean lines between music and cooking, the written word and sex, or the smartphone and a melon. Look closely, explore widely, and you can't help but connect all these things to one another, if only loosely. And those connections ensure even the smallest action has the potential to become the proverbial flapping of butterfly wings that causes a typhoon on the other side of the planet.

Progress is similarly intertwined. And that means we're only truly moving forward, evolving in a positive fashion, when we're aware of the negative consequences of our growth, of the places, people, and realms of thought that suffer when others flourish.

Progress is ideally counterbalanced, I think, with a certain amount of conservatism. I don't use these words in the political sense, but in the sense of there being people who are focused on progress at all costs, and those who are more concerned with keeping things stable and secure.

Societies that celebrate both ends of the spectrum, and all the gradients of gray in between, tend to enjoy the best of both worlds. They benefit from those who shout for more, for better, for improvements upon that which we already have. But they also benefit from those who are saying, hold on, let's slow down for a minute here and take stock, let's make sure none of what we've already built crumbles around us while we're trying to build this new thing, okay?

Balance is key. It's easy to become an extremist, in how we act, in what we believe, in the ideologies to which we adhere. Balance, on the other hand, requires we adjust our weight back and forth, between competing ideas that are in many cases zero-sum. The resources used for technological evolution cannot be designated for bridge repair. Recognizing that people using new technologies will probably be better off with fully functioning, safe bridges is key to establishing this balance societally. Recognizing that we may be able to evolve our bridges with what we learn from our research is also important.

This same balancing act takes place inside each of us as individuals, and within our societies. Understanding this is key to ensuring we don't wobble out of balance, losing the benefits of steady movement across a stable foundation.

Questions To Ask

Questions are often more valuable to the depth and value of a conversation than statements. Speaking declaratively is useful for cobbling together things you've already learned, but to ensure you're saying things that make sense, and that you receive the right information from others, you have to ask the right questions. And many of us are never taught how to do this.

Many of us lack the questioning reflex because propriety steals it from us as we grow up. It's not polite to ask. Or it may be the wrong time, and you don't want to be rude. If you ask questions, you'll show your ignorance, and others will judge you. Perhaps you've been taught to stick to the surface, the superficial, never going deeper than headlines and slogans and talking points with any issue, leaving the more fundamental currents and riptides and important-but-uncomfortable details largely unexplored.

It's understandable, then, that we might be nearly incapable of confidently questioning by the time we become adults. We've been fed enough information to feel we understand things, and we've had our realities shaped so that politeness, propriety, tradition, and a respect for authority keeps us from looking too closely at the things we know. This makes us easier to lead, but it doesn't make us terribly responsible citizenry. It's prudent to keep one's head down and toe the line under authoritarian regimes that punish dissenters and troublemakers. But in societies in which we have the right to challenge, to disagree, to speak our minds, to rabble-rouse and demand change, it's almost insulting to those who won us these rights, and who have fought to uphold them over the generations, for us to sit back and meekly accept explanations that are demonstrably false.

Those who are capable of questioning and do not question will eventually find they cannot. That shift may only arrive later, impacting their descendants rather than themselves, but the trend still holds that societies which fail to be engaged at the individual level, and which fail to make use of the rights afforded them, not only fail to acquire new rights over time, but generally lose the ones they have. There's incentive for people in power to extricate rights from others while increasing their own, as it allows them to more easily acquire more power and defend that which they already have. It's by questioning—by always demanding answers and holding those who answer accountable for falsehoods—that we ensure future generations are more liberated, rather than less.

But which questions to ask? How do we even get started questioning the world around us? Which fundamentals should we be looking at and wondering about? What is a useful question, and what's not?

I would argue the only useless question is one with an answer you don't understand and then fail to follow up on, not pursuing further information or asking supplementary questions. It's a sad state of affairs when data is available to us but we lack the wherewithal to utilize it. Without a foundational body of knowledge at our disposal, we're unlikely to be able to put new information into context, and as such will be unable to distinguish its truth or falsehood, or understand its utility and meaning.

I suppose another useless question would be one asked of the wrong person, or one that is asked not in good faith, but used as a sharp object to prod at someone with whom you disagree. There's absolutely a use for uncomfortable questions forcing the acknowledgement of some misdeed or mistake, as such questions allow us to clarify what happened. But a question that forces someone to answer in a way that muddies the truth, or that has bias in the question itself, is more a stunt than a pursuit of knowledge. The famous, "Have you stopped beating your wife?" is an example of a loaded question that, although in the most literal sense is probably a good thing to get straight, in the way it's typically used—to set someone up so that no matter how they answer, it appears as though they did something they did not—is a tool for gaining leverage or to embarrass, not to gain knowledge or inform.

Most other questions, though, are valuable in some way. I look to children for inspiration in this regard, because implied societal norms can be debilitating. We feel as if it's impolite, embarrassing, or weird in some unquantifiable way to ask questions, even simple ones, of someone with whom we're interacting. This carries over even to places where the whole point is asking questions: during a Q&A session after a book reading, during a press junket at a political rally, with a philosopher who you randomly meet at a coffee shop.

In each case, we come up with rational-seeming excuses as to why we don't question as much as we might like to. During Q&A sessions and press junkets, we want to make sure everyone has a turn and don't want to stand out as that annoying person with all the questions. While chatting at the coffee shop, we don't want to take up too much of the other person's time, or don't feel it's an appropriate setting for a long, involved dive into big topics.

By the rules of civility and caring about other peoples' time and attention, this is absolutely true in some cases. But more often than we'd think, those politicians would love the opportunity to get into the nitty-gritty details of the education plan they spent so much time refining. But they need someone to ask them about it, and to ask the right followup questions. I can say, as an author who regularly tours and does Q&A sessions after my readings, I love it when there are engaged people in the audience who ask deeper or wider questions which allow me to expound on my prior answer, and which challenge me to really think and explain more thoroughly my experiences or ideas about a given topic. Ideally they allow other people to have the chance, as well, but there are often moments of dead silence during these sessions that would likely be filled if only the curious and interested would bypass the social misgivings they feel and ask what they want to ask.

The same is true of engaging with someone over coffee. It may be that they'd prefer to be left alone, and just want to sit and think without interruption. But if you pay attention to their nonverbal and spoken cues, you should be able to pick up on whether that's the case, or if they're interested in expounding on their ideas for a while, if only someone would ask them the right questions.

In some cases, your questions, asked from an outside perspective and by someone who has a different collection of facts and experiences to draw from, allows the person you're asking to see something new, to recognize a new angle of something they were working on. Maybe they'll come up with a new method of explaining a complex idea, or simply refine an existing one, whittling away the parts that obfuscate and emphasizing the pieces that illuminate.

When trying to decide which questions to ask and how to ask them, watch to see how kids do it.

Children haven't yet adopted the social niceties of the adults around them, and as such, almost compulsively seek out new information about the world around them. When they're babies, this means touching and tasting and sniffing everything they can get their hands on. Once they're capable of speaking, though, that predisposition becomes an ongoing game of, "Why?"

Why do ladybugs have spots? Why are your socks that color? Why does that man have such a long beard? Why don't you have a long beard? Why are some people mean? Why are the clouds that shape? Why can't I stay up and play more games? Why can't I dress the dog up in your clothes? Why do I have to eat peas? Why are you being so unfair?

Anything and everything is on the table. I imagine the always-on questions can grate on a person over the span of months and years, but I can't help but appreciate the brazenness of this approach. Kids are biologically driven to seek out information about their environments. This is what helps them survive, but it's also what fills up their brains, which start out empty of data to use in making decisions and understanding how the world works, but which very quickly contain enough information for them to become real people, full human beings with opinions and perspectives. A dearth of data will not prevent them from forming their own opinions, of course—the world is full of adults who have very strong opinions based on very little information—but children who saturate themselves with data and experiences usually have a more accurate, complete idea of how the world works and what connects to what, which is a huge advantage.

To question, then, is natural. It's fundamental to who we are as thinking, sentient creatures. It's our equivalent of being taken out hunting by the adults of the pack. We don't sharpen our teeth, we sharpen our minds.

Note that children don't restrict themselves to asking

questions about things they perceive to be valuable. Rare are the toddlers that follow their parents around, asking how to manage an investment portfolio or how to get more ROI from marketing to their audience. Kids don't yet have a hardened, concrete understanding of what's valuable, and as such, are free to question the world liberally: spreading their attention widely, gorging on data about things that we adults consider important, but also on things that we perceive to be superfluous. Is it vital that they know why ladybugs have spots? This is the sort of question that would sound strange coming from an adult, but the answer can take us down a circuitous, many-tiered path to understanding bugs, biology, the history of exploration, and the scientific method. Valueless questions, then, can often be those that, if properly pursued, result in the most value. Kids don't ask these questions because they seek enlightenment, but their predisposition for asking helps them achieve it latently. We as adults require rationales for doing things, and for me, this childish approach is a powerful excuse to ask questions about seemingly useless things. It helps me acquire valuable knowledge I didn't know enough to recognize as valuable.

The way we ask questions will ideally be similarly assertive and persistent. Again, kids are well known for the agony they cause their parents, asking not just one question, but a flurry of twenty, each one going a little deeper than the last, until at some point the parent gives up, frustratedly providing them with a non-answer: "That's just how it is," or "Because I said so."

This is the standard, fictional depiction of how these conversations work, at least. I'm guessing a lot of parents and other adults who have children in their lives gamely follow up, providing as much additional context as they can, answering until the kid becomes distracted by something else, or until they, themselves, have to check a higher reference, whipping out the encyclopedia, Googling, or taking the child to the library to find a book on the subject.

Ideally, this is exactly how we respond to our own questions, whether asked of someone else or posited internally. I can't tell you how many times a seemingly innocuous question about why an ingredient is used a certain way in a recipe has led me down a rabbit hole. Seven or eight Wikipedia pages later, I've come to understand how antacids work, why acoustic cavitation is an important concept in the field of energy production, and the historical significance of a master sauce.

We typically stop, though, once we discover a practical answer to a simple question. Why is it sometimes better to use frozen butter when baking a pastry? Oh, because it causes the scones to be puffier when they're done. Knowledge acquired. Back to doing things.

There's nothing wrong with this method of pursuit, but it can be limiting, because it derails our curiosity right at the moment when we're most open to new information. I could stop there, but why not click on a few more links, ask a few more questions? For instance: why does frozen butter cause the pastry to have a different texture? Is there another way to accomplish the same? How do different cultures accomplish this in their regional cuisines? Is the same true of butter-substitutes, or is there something about butter in particular that makes this occur?

There are countless directions to wander in the pursuit of any answer, and sticking to just one is practical in the sense of getting that one thing and then going back to whatever it was you were doing that sparked the question, but impractical in that it limits you to just that one path, and prevents you from stumbling upon answers to questions you wouldn't have otherwise thought to ask.

Children are able to learn and understand so quickly

because they graze widely on a variety of topics. They collect bits and pieces from all over the intellectual map and weave them together into an expansive web of knowledge, filling in the gaps as they grow. Mono-focused kids would be at a significant disadvantage, as they may be limited in their overall range of future options, and they may have no context in which to place that one thing they know about. As a result, they wouldn't necessarily understand why they performed the actions they performed. They would go through the motions, but lack any understanding as to why.

Does that sound familiar at all? I've known many adults who do exactly that: performing the same motions every day, uncertain as to why these actions are necessary or done the way they are. The steps they're supposed to take have been memorized and even optimized, but the reason for those steps, and any potential alternatives to them, are completely out of reach.

It's questioning that allows us to identify those alternatives. It's context that gives us the freedom to understand where we fit amidst everything and everyone else. It allows us to understand what role we play and what role we could play.

Questions help us suss out the truths behind the actions of others, and trace back to the source of seemingly random events. We can assess a complex web of why's and how's and figure out who benefits, why it happened now, what's changed, and whether or not the information we're receiving is legitimate. We can analyze the bias in what we're told, and meta-analyze our own bias in how we perceive it.

We can decide whether to act, or whether action is inadvisable. We can determine which actions to take, and how to align those actions with what we believe, knowing what we know about the situation and about ourselves.

Knowledge is vital. Asking questions is how we achieve that vitality.

Choosing A Metric

We measure much of what happens in the world, how successful a person is, how well we're doing and even feeling using a single metric.

Money is wonderful. I'm not going to tap-dance around that. Currency has allowed us to aggregate effort and build up networks of interconnected people capable of building amazing things since its inception. There are broad benefits to other methods of value exchange, but money is by far the most accessible, practical, and convenient means of doing so. This is increasingly the case as we've moved from shells to coins to paper bills to digital currency. Each step along the way has represented less infrastructural cost and increased stability for the system it supports.

Money is often a stand-in for other types of conflict. Throughout history it's been money or guns (or the contemporary death-machine equivalent) that have been the spear-point of power, and though it's not always pleasant when someone buys up and gentrifies a neighborhood, it's substantially better than having them roll through, kill all the locals, and take it by force.

It makes sense, then, that we would place a great deal of

intellectual and social emphasis on money. It's a proxy for many other types of value, and the common metric by which we can assess the worth of almost anything.

This is how it works in theory, at least. In practice, money has been abused, its potency as an unbiased metric watered-down, its utility as a peacemaker and value-broker defaced by asterisks. Yes, money is still all the things it once was, but it's also the tool, and in some cases the weapon, of those who have learned to take advantage of the system it has helped build. It's manipulatable by those with a certain type of education and background. It's inheritable in a way that other types of power in the past have not been, which in turn, over time, amasses power in families and other small groups who have not earned it.

As an omni-metric, a unit of measurement we use for everything, money has become mutated and of dubious value. Did the person with all the digits in their bank account earn their fortune by exchanging value they created for wealth gladly traded by others? Or did they inherit it or cleverly take it in some way, perhaps manipulating markets or day trading or otherwise taking advantage of a system which they cynically see themselves as separate from and above?

Money works well when we're all beholden to the same rules, and when the complexities that have empowered its utility are not used against the very system of value upon which it's predicated. Unfortunately, the world we live in is largely owned and operated by those who have learned to manipulate that system, which places increasingly more power and value, unearned though it might be, in their hands.

Due to the nature of this system, we often see these system-abusers in the same light in which we might see someone who has created a great deal of value for the world. The millionaire day trader is not immediately and obviously different from the millionaire technologist who invented a device which has saved millions of lives. The market doesn't differentiate between the two, and society, as both the parent and intellectual byproduct of the market, celebrates both as heroes, doing the former too much justice and the latter not enough.

This warps our perception of goodness. Of social value. The result is that instead of working to make positive change, to do good, we seek out the assumed consequence of those acts: we seek out money. To people who have no reason to differentiate between money earned in different ways, this means if we can find a clever way to extract money from the system, even if we don't create anything of value, or we sap value from society in the process, we're still doing it right. We're still superstars.

Capitalism is predicated on the idea that money works, exchange works, a unified value metric works, because it incentivizes us to create valuable things. The result, then, should be an ever-increasing amount of value for all, because our societies are predicated on reward systems that divvy out value to those who contribute the same.

The version of capitalism that has become dominant around the world does not line up with this ideal. It's perpetuated by people who extract rather than contribute. There are still successful people who add to the pot before taking a big handful out, but they are increasingly the exception rather than the rule. Those with the most wealth are often those who have come up with ways to take without giving, or to take far more than they give. Because that's how you "win" in the sense of having more of the currency by which we gauge success than other people.

The big picture problem here is that the system of organization around which everything we do orbits, is both corrupted and corrupting. This system also forms the foundation for how we measure our own success and gauge how "good" we are according to the moral terms of the society in which we live.

On an individual level, the consequences of this relationship are immense and omnipresent.

From a young age, we're funneled through rites of upbringing and education that revolve around the flawed economics of some local flavor of crony capitalism. We come to understand that money is good and not having money is bad. If we don't have money, we can't live—we will actually die from lack of food and shelter—so money is important. It's the most important thing.

As we grow into adults who care about things like self-actualization and happiness defined by metrics not found the color-within-the-lines manuals we've been provided, we still often limit ourselves to defining happiness in economic terms. If I can make this much money each month, I can leave this soul-sucking job I hate. If I can reduce my expenses, I won't need to work so much and can free up time to spend on that hobby I've been neglecting. If I invest properly now, I may be able to not work at all at some point in the distant future.

Both our survival instincts, and our sentient drive for meaning, then, are tied up in this single metric. Money has come to represent not just valuable, exchangeable objects, but anything we might value. Our time, our ability to live life on our terms. Until we have enough money, we can't say or do anything that might cause us to get fired. Our ability to think and have opinions for ourselves, then, is also tied to money.

Despite its ubiquity, and despite its overwhelming influence on essentially every aspect of life, money is not the only metric by which we can measure these things. It's the default metric, the one we're taught to respect and pursue, and it's interconnected with all the other metrics we might discover in often disconcerting ways. But it's not the only one. And it's not even the best one, in some cases.

Allow me to present an alternative view of money and its role in human society.

Consider that, to survive, to continue existing from one second to the next, you need air. Breathable air with the right amount of nitrogen, oxygen, argon, and trace amounts of other gases is a requisite for survival. Without that, no quantity of any other resources matters much, because you will not exist to utilize them.

Consider, too, that food, the energy we use to keep our bodies functioning, is a necessity of life. Even if we have air and money, without food we're doomed. Our brains will shut down and our hearts will stop pumping blood.

Now, if you have plenty of air to breathe—as much as you need, but no more than that—and you meet a man who has a great abundance of air, perhaps he owns enough air for a billion people, what would you think about that man?

Not much at all, probably. I mean, it's interesting that he owns air, I guess, but what possible meaning would we ascribe to that ownership? Why is it important? We need enough air to survive, to keep our internal processes operating at peak effectiveness. But beyond that, of what value is more air?

Now think about the same example, but with food. Imagine you have enough food to be full at all times. You couldn't possibly eat any more than you already own if you tried, not without getting sick. You have enough to keep going, to keep your organs happy, your brain fueled, your health maintained. And then you meet a man who has a billion times more food than he needs, than he could ever consume. What do you think of this man?

If you're living in a time of scarcity, you're maybe thinking he has the ability to do a lot of good, to feed a lot of people. But if we're imagining we live in a time where everyone has the same amount of food as we do, exactly the right amount, then this guy with this stockpile seems a little strange, yes? What reason could he possibly have for collecting all this spare food he'll never need?

Keep these examples in mind as you think about meaning and purpose and happiness.

We live in a world in which we're all trying to stockpile as much of the things we need and think we need as possible. But in many cases, arguably most cases, we also pursue a great deal of excess that we demonstrably don't need. There's good reason to want to have enough air to breathe and it's an excellent idea to ensure you have enough food to stay alive and healthy. But to stockpile, to hoard, to take and take and take way beyond what's necessary for optimal personal function is obscene. There's an evolutionary argument for our propensity to do this, because we want to ensure that if our food supply disappears we've got extra available. But although we still feel the drive to accumulate endlessly, without an off-switch that triggers when we reach the point of ridiculousness, this pursuit doesn't add anything to our lives. The time and energy we spend aiming to have a billion spare supplies of air does not make us any happier, healthier, or more oxygenated. All it does is take up space and consume other resources that are far more finite.

Time, for instance, is that rare resource of which we can never get more, and which we can actually benefit from caching and protecting. More time means more of whatever we like, and so long as the bare necessities—air, food, shelter —are taken care of, we're in a good spot to pursue higher needs, like intellectual fulfillment, moral growth, and personal happiness.

Accumulating other types of resources does not afford us the same. More food than we need does not liberate us in any way. More breathable air than we can ever inhale does not expand our minds. More money than we could ever spend does not make us better people.

Having just enough food, just enough air, and just enough money, though, is a potent combination. It's an equation that is almost shockingly simple, and yet all too often ignored. It's also the rare formula that, when worked out intentionally with a focus on our individual priorities, liberates more of our time. It grants us access to a larger percentage of that singular resource we can never get more of once it's spent. This, in turn, increases the chances that in the time we have between birth and death, we will experience more happiness and satisfaction than sadness and discontent.

Focusing on the important stuff, the vital, allows you to more effectively divvy out your time and energy so you spend just the right amount of it in pursuit of the resources that allow you to survive and thrive, but no more than that.

To accomplish this, we require some sense of self-awareness. We need to understand who we are and what we actually care about. We have to be able to consciously, and regularly, step back from the minutiae of everyday life to look at the big picture, to ascertain what's working and what's not, what we'd like to have more of and what we could safely and happily go without.

By reframing life in this way, and reworking our priorities as a result, we're less tethered to a system of corrupt people and corruptible values. We're still inextricably connected to that system, but we can live in a way that makes us less dependent on it, increasing our chances of achieving success and fulfillment according to our personal standards.

Money isn't evil, nor are people who have it. Not even the people who corrupt our system of currencies and exchange are evil: they're simply acting rationally within a system that incentivizes them to act in a particular way. They may be acting thoughtlessly, but that's not an indication of their absolute values. If provided an alternative they could see and understand, I'm guessing a whole lot of them would run for the hills, gleefully leaving behind their stockpiles in favor of something more tailored and less gluttonous.

And though they're also not evil, the systems that incentivize us to see money as the be-all, end-all, and encourage us to base our sense of morality on acquiring more money are harmful to our priorities and needs. These systems can be useful, and it's valuable to understand how they operate and how to operate within them: if you don't have a fundamental understanding of how to earn money, how to spend it, and how to avoid being taken advantage of, you're likely to fall prey to someone who's far savvier and who can use your ignorance against you.

If you can learn enough about money to survive and earn a sufficient amount to fund your ambitions, then, you'll be in an advantageous position to accomplish goals that are meaningful to you.

Internationality

From time immemorial, little has been more exciting and potentially dangerous than the strange group of people who live on the other side of the lake. Or over the mountain range. Or in the next valley. Or across the ocean.

The borders we've drawn around our societies are imaginary and only exist in the sense that we agree they do. As a consequence of those borders, however, we've built real barriers and structures along them, and invented laws that designate how we should respond if someone crosses them without permission. But these borders are not inevitable; they are not how things have always been and are not necessarily how they'll always be. Borders have waxed and waned throughout history, and the concept of Westphalian Sovereignty, of respecting each other's borders, is a relatively recent one. It only emerged in 1648, and was named after the Treaty of Westphalia, which ended the massive European Thirty Years' War. It was an attempt to enforce peace despite ideological disagreement and geographic adjacency.

Before that treaty, borders were a lot more fluid. They certainly existed: these lords would tell these other lords to stay the hell away from their crops, and would perch troops in

190

little camps and bunkers throughout the region they perceived to be theirs. But the other groups in the area might also consider some of that land to be theirs, and would roll out their own troops, their own camps, and their own fortifications. Many tiny conflicts would ensue, and the assumed borders would change for a while, but only until the next scuffle.

Since the Treaty of Westphalia, territories have been a lot more rigid. The advent of internationally accepted borders means we are less likely to disagree about where one country ends and another begins, today, which in turn means the border scuffles of yore have become quite rare, taking place only in relatively new contested regions, such as Kashmir, between Pakistan and India, and the South China Sea, between China and essentially everyone else in the region. Boldly stepping in and taking land is an act that has been relegated to larger scale conflicts, which are far more rare than minor land-grabs and counter-offensives. The costs of war are much higher for everyone involved these days, and as such, the benefits of instigating one are almost always outweighed by the downsides.

That said, a great deal of rearranging does tend to take place post-conflict, and the Balkanization of a region—that is, intentionally dividing it up, post-war, so the new states are all unlikely to get along with each other, creating continuous conflict and, resultantly, non-cooperation—has become common. The Ottoman Empire was one of the first modern empires to be shattered and Balkanized (which is where we get that term, for the Balkans region in what was formerly the Southwest Ottoman Empire) into the many smaller and oppositional states that make up Central Europe and the Middle East, today. The same happened to the territory held by the Third Reich after World War II. This intentional fracturing of a group of people is intended to keep them divided, and serves this purpose well.

The term Balkanization is also, in a more modern context, sometimes used to describe the potential strength of regions that are kept intentionally separated but which still work well together; societies that benefit from their differences while still maintaining a loose, regional unity.

By this definition, the states that make up the United States are somewhat Balkanized, though the increased and increasing powers of the central, federal government reduces the potential benefits of this a little. The United Kingdom might be a better example, as there are complex but largely beneficial laws that define the relationships between the semi-autonomous regions of England, Scotland, Wales, and Northern Ireland, in addition to neighboring Ireland, the nearby Isle of Man, and the loosely tied collection of 52 Commonwealth member states around the world that were the result of Britain's 20th century decolonization.

The benefits of positive Balkanization are that you can allow different groups to operate by different rules, while still enjoying many of the benefits of a larger, more unified population.

You could have a country of 100 million people, all operating by the same laws, paying the same taxes, adhering to roughly the same cultural standards. Or you could have two countries, each containing 50 million people, and each operating with different tax codes, different laws, and developing unique cultures of their own. They perhaps have alliances and trade deals that make working together mutually beneficial, and because they have two different modes of operation, they have a great deal more to share with each other: different music and art, different technological developments that are common in one region but not in the other, perhaps educational institutions flourish on one side of the border while they're crippled on the other, but that crippling is the consequence of less stringent educational requirements that afford the locals other benefits. The idea is that both groups are better off because they have a strong relationship with a nearby society that does things differently than they do things.

If both countries were identical, there wouldn't be as many benefits, and you might as well just be the same country and save on bureaucratic and infrastructural costs. But by loosely connecting different countries, both are free to regulate and legislate as they please, and to create their own cultures, while also enjoying some of the advantages from across the border.

This is what the ideal situation would look like, at least. On a real-world stage, it's seldom two countries of equal size we're talking about, and instead a widely varying collection of 200 different societies, and maybe half of them have regularly worked together in varying ways, to varying degrees, in the 20th century.

There are some cynical, political reasons to create organizations like the United Nations. They help enforce current economic and military dominance, for instance, increasing the might of those already in control. But the UN is also one of the biggest and most successful alliances in history, tethering together 193 nations so we can, in ways big and small, benefit from each other's presence. In some cases this means trade deals that incentivize cross-border economic activity. Sometimes it means visa arrangements that make it easier for groups to journey to foreign lands, soaking up their culture, buying their stuff, meeting their people, and attending their schools. Often it just means having a central meeting point where we can work out our disagreements non-militarily, so we're less likely to go to war with each other; a particularly prudent concern in the nuclear age.

The UN and groups like it, though, are still primarily intended as solutions to the larger problem that we're still, as a species, utterly fixated on tribalism.

Tribalism is an upgraded version of the pack hunting seen in many kinds of animal. It allows us to work together, and in turn, to achieve a lot more than we would alone or as smaller, family units.

In the past, this meant mutual protection, and the ability to tackle a woolly mammoth, rather than sticking to hunting rabbits. Today, it still means mutual protection, but it also means dividing the world into Us and Them, carving out divisions so we can better identify who to protect and who we need to be protected from.

These divisions can be racial, they can be religious, they can be regional, or they can be completely fabricated from nothing at all. One of the requirements of having a tribe, though, is having a group of people who are with you while everyone else is not. If we embraced an ideology that centered around us all being human first with all the other differences mattering very little, our tribe would likely be too large to psychologically manage and control. As a result, we imbue small things that matter very little in practice with increased significance; we intellectualize these things into mattering a great deal.

The group across the lake is very tall while we, on this side, are very short. It must be bad to be tall; those idiots probably blow over in the wind. They give up strength and brains in exchange for extra vertical inches. They are less than us. Almost animals, really. We should watch out for them. Maybe kill them if they step out of line.

Throughout history, the divisions we've decided are vital have been as superficial as the average height between groups or the general difference in skin tone. These differences are the consequence of genetic variation and sequestration, not inherent superiority or inferiority, but that doesn't stop us from deciding that one skin color is better, one height is better, one cultural lineage is better.

None of these differences make one group inherently superior, but we decide they do because we need to feel we're on the winning team, and that our group has something special worth defending. A genetic or cultural disposition that encouraged its bearers to feel inferior to everyone else wouldn't last long. The bearers of such genes would simply give up their distinctiveness to join another group, or maybe give up, seeing no reason to try to compete with the people across the lake.

The groups that survive, then, are those which feel they have something going for them, some kind of genetic, spiritual, or cultural superiority. Tribalism helped our ancestors work together, support each other, and grow into societies, rather than mere collections of individuals.

Today, unfortunately, this propensity toward tribalism is part of what's kept us from more resiliently unifying our diverse groups in a mutually beneficial fashion. The benefits of internationalism, of becoming more globalized, are massive and measurable. But the pushback against this, the movements from all sides of the political spectrum and in cultures all around the world, continue to keep this from happening. The tribalism that has always helped us in the past now limits us, and makes us distrustful, fearful, and regressive when it comes to dealing with groups beyond our own.

Sometimes this ideology takes the shape of outright xenophobia and racism. Sometimes it's subtler, and instead wears the guise of patriotism. "America first" is something I hear a lot in the United States, and though it's a better statement than "American only," it's still a harmful sentiment if we hope to create a global human network. People in the US should be taken care of, certainly, but to paint our relationships in those terms implies we have to be utterly selfish and introverted in our dealings with others, when in fact, being more open and generous will bear much greater fruit. That sharing our strengths and celebrating the strengths of others is somehow detrimental to our well-being is an ignorant idea easily sold to a mistrustful populace. Globalization has become a word with negative connotations, but the process of globalizing has brought more benefits to more people than almost any other effort in human history, and we haven't come close to reaching its full potential.

If two countries with 50 million people apiece can benefit from their diversity and proximity, due to trade and cultural exchange, imagine what seven billion, and growing, people in 200-ish nations can gain from their relationships with each other. We're not just talking about fusion cuisine and the translation of books into other languages; we're looking at the potential to share our perspectives, our technological and manufacturing capabilities, our education systems, and our genetic distinctiveness.

That last point is a good metaphor for all the others, actually: a diverse genetic pool makes a species more resilient. A "pure" genetic group is more likely to die off from disease, to succumb to gene-embedded conditions, to fail to evolve as the environment around them evolves. Diversity is a strength but we treat it as a weakness.

We have the opportunity, due to our immense communication capabilities and our travel and trade networks, to build a human union unlike anything seen before. We have the ability to maintain our cultural differences, and embrace them, becoming more Us than ever before, while still sharing what we do well with the rest of the world, with the rest of our globe-spanning species.

We have the opportunity to ensure this network of nations operates like a well-balanced ecosystem, with a great deal of beneficial interconnectedness that ensures all groups have valuable roles to play and have the mutual support of all other groups. The more we rely on each other, the less likely we are to find reason to kill each other, or to consider the group across the border inferior because they're different. We'll know and respect their value. We'll also know and respect our own.

Right now, in the early 21st century, as a surge of local-first movements swells around the world, it's difficult to imagine how such a system might be implemented, much less survive and thrive. I don't believe that the ideas behind these local-first movements are inherently oppositional to a larger, more sustainable and beneficial ecosystem, but it does require a reframing.

Focusing on the local is important. If we haven't taken care of our own neighborhoods, we don't stand much chance of contributing in any meaningful way to our larger city, state, or country. Going one step further, we have to take care of ourselves, ensuring we are each physically, economically, and psychologically stable, with excess to give, before we're in optimal shape to contribute beyond ourselves.

From the very smallest unit to the largest, then, it's vital we focus on the foundation and build up from there. Many of us, in a very humanitarian, good-intentioned way, fail to take care of ourselves before we expand and scale up. We might give everything to our culture, for instance, but in doing so become shells of ourselves, lacking the time, energy, and resources to become individually fulfilled and to grow.

More ideally, we take the time to become the best possible versions of ourselves, first, and share the excess with our communities, with our cultures, and with other cultures outside of our own.

Start small, stabilize, flourish, and grow. Repeat this process until we're all capable of not just imagining a larger world, but playing a role in it. Sustaining it. Helping it grow sustainably as we ourselves already have.

Fragile individuals have trouble imagining anything but a fragile world. We owe it to ourselves to make sure everything is good inside ourselves and at home, and ideally that reinforcement and growth becomes a step on the path toward something bigger.

Ideals & Realities

The term "ivory tower" refers to people or institutions that pursue knowledge or enlightenment while separated from the real-world applications and implications of their pursuits.

Politicians who decide what health care their citizenry will receive while they enjoy the maximum possible care either way could be said to live in an ivory tower. The world around them, the choices made, the practical realities other people face do not touch them. And yet they see fit to make decisions about that reality as if they know firsthand what they're talking about.

It's possible to understand things in the abstract. To understand, intellectually, things like war, even if you've never been in one. With a great deal of research and perhaps talking to people who have experienced combat, you may come to grasp the matter sufficiently that you're able to make decisions about it.

The same is true in other aspects of life. We needn't work in a butcher shop to infer the outlines, and even some of the texture and color, of what happens inside that shop, up front and in the back. We can then pull smells, tastes, sounds from other relevant experiences to decide whether or not we want to work in one. Cobbling together relevant information in this way doesn't result in a 100% accurate impression of what takes place in such a space—the details will inevitably be blurry, and many of them wrong—but it's often enough that we can paint a mental picture, allowing us to discuss butcher shops without needing to be inside one as we do so.

There are still cases in which it's prudent to have firsthand knowledge, despite our ability to imagine and estimate. You can make decisions about which equipment to order for a butcher shop in which you've invested by reading reviews and looking at the pictures and descriptions in catalogs. But you'd probably be better served if you allow the folks who actually work there, who have hands-on experience with these different manufacturers and devices, to make that choice. There are times when floating above a situation allows you to see more and, understanding the larger context, bring something valuable to the table. At other times, having boots on the ground and hands on the equipment is required for optimal decision-making.

A major criticism about universities, and university living in particular, is that they pull students from the real world into an ivory tower, where they learn about things in the abstract but often fail to connect those ideas and ideals with concrete reality.

Imagine a class discussion about communism as a governmental system, for instance. I personally recall several in-class instances of fellow students declaring that communism is clearly better than the system to which we adhere, and that red history is full of heroes who only cared for the people and wanted to pull down tyrants, but the capitalist pigs murdered them to ensure the protection of their ill-gotten power.

There are good arguments to be made for the many economic and governing systems that have emerged throughout history, including communism. But the boots-on-the-ground reality of that particular system, historically, has been communism-branded dictatorial regimes. Stalin and Mao committed some of the greatest atrocities in history. The theoretical ideal of what a communist government should be clashes dramatically with the real-world examples we've seen.

I believe it is a privilege to have the time to think about butcher shops and communist governments from a safe distance. Not because it's an inherently better situation, but because it gives us time to exercise our imaginations and consider broader scopes and scales. This is difficult to do once you're down in the midst of things, focusing on staying afloat, with little time and energy to spare for those bigger, nonessential-seeming issues. It's harder to see the forest when you're surrounded by trees.

Philosophical rumination is essential, even though it won't help you pay the bills. Scientific inquiry is essential, even if it won't protect you from victimization. These ivory tower values are not at all necessary to survive, but they are, I would argue, integrally connected to everything we do. If we value them and utilize them, they enable us to amplify all our efforts. Combined with ground-level experience, the overhead view is even more valuable. And vice versa.

But access to this ability to step away, step aside, step into a world where intellectual pursuit is an end unto itself, is a privilege. It's an advantage that isn't afforded to most people on the planet and as such it's prudent to remember that if we're given the opportunity, we shouldn't squander it. Most ideally, when we're doing our thinking, when we're ruminating about governmental systems, when we're deciding who gets what type of healthcare, we should remember that most people are not us. Not everyone has the same access, the same resources, and yes, the same lofty perspective as those of us who have been allowed inside the tower. Not everyone has the good fortune to have the time to sit and think and not die if they make the wrong choice.

The overhead view is just a different view. It allows us to see different things, but also the same things as everyone else from a different angle. The elevated point of view isn't the right one, or the only one. It's best when mixed with side and bottom perspectives, which are achieved at ground level, and by moving around, standing in different places, thinking different thoughts.

A dedication to achieving three-dimensionality in our observations allows us to make better choices. It allows us to see that although this new technology will increase manufacturing output by 50%, it will also eliminate half the jobs in the industry. In the long-term this may be wonderful, provided the long-term either opens up new jobs for those otherwise unemployed workers, or we establish a new system where those lost paychecks aren't necessary for the people who currently require them to live.

In the short-term, though, this victory for manufacturing is a death knell for a large number of people. People who, perhaps, don't have that same overhead view, who don't have the ability or desire to see beyond the daily commute and at-work responsibilities, but people who matter nonetheless. Recognizing this can help alleviate some of the most harmful effects of the ivory tower. The big picture ideally emphasizes the human benefits of the long-term and doesn't diminish the suffering of those who will pay for those changes in the immediate future.

Privilege, be it the privilege of being able to go to a university or the privilege of having happened to be born of a certain race or gender or economic status, is something that's difficult to see if you have it. It's natural to assume that if you succeed more frequently than others, or if you have access to more resources than others, well, it's because you're just that good. It would be intellectually harmful to assume that everything you have is the consequence of outside forces, of luck, rather than your own hard work. Thus, those who have advantages tend to assume that these are the consequence of their abilities and effort, and nothing more.

This is sometimes the case, of course, but to a lesser degree than we tend to assume. Hard work and ability go a long way, but when not paired with infrastructural advantage, they're just as likely to result in little or nothing as they are to push a person forward in life.

Something that strikes me every time I visit a city like Kolkata in India, where poverty levels are sky-high and the infrastructure is massively degraded, is that there are so many incredibly intelligent, wildly capable people living there. I can easily imagine many of them doing big things, earning tons of money, developing valuable new ways of thinking, running big companies or organizations, except that they were born into a situation that makes these things unlikely. These are some of the most skilled and driven people I've met anywhere on the planet, but because they don't have firm ground to stand on, don't have reliable sources of food and potable water, don't have reliable access to things like electricity and the internet, they're not able to utilize these gifts in the same way someone born middle class in the United States might be able to. I would guess that someone born middle class in the US, and who had far less natural capability, would probably achieve a whole lot more than most of these brilliant, relatively impoverished people, simply because of their circumstances.

This is a tough pill to swallow. We're primed to believe that capability and hard work rises to the top. This is the motivating force behind a lot of our efforts: we work harder, we earn more, we gain more respect and credibility, and we have better lives. Unfortunately, it's not a one-to-one conversion, and some people are born with thumbs on the scale.

Having been born white, male, straight, middle class, healthy, with a loving family and a United States passport, I have a huge advantage in many aspects of life. Working hard, learning as much as possible, and creating things I think are valuable still matters, but those latent advantages amplify anything I do.

Most people have advantages of some kind, whether they're immediately apparent or not. Maybe their advantages are only relevant in some circumstances, and maybe they're intrinsically tied to disadvantages in other areas of life. Whatever the specifics, it's valuable to recognize this is the case. Not because we should feel guilty about having certain advantages and privileges, but because it allows us to see the world more clearly. To better understand how it works, and the people in it.

It's valuable to recognize, for instance, that someone who does not have as much money as I have may not be lazy or incapable. Their circumstances may be the result of certain disadvantages, rather than personal attitude or aptitude. Someone with more money than me isn't inherently more skilled or intelligent, and doesn't necessarily produce more value than I do. They may simply have been born into circumstances that gave them a head start: family with money, better education, valuable connections, and so on.

For most of history, and still today, many groups have had their work stolen by members of other groups who are considered to be more legitimate. In the United States, for instance, this has generally meant white guys. A great deal of work done by minorities and women has been attributed to white, male managers or counterparts. When trying to figure out why there aren't as many black women in managerial positions in certain industries, then, we have things to consider beyond mere capability. Is it because they lack the desire or skill to make it in that field? Or is it a reflection of the privilege that has been traditionally enjoyed by some and not by others in that industry?

Historical context matters. Being able to see the impact of what's happened in the past, today, matters. Recognizing that we all have different starting points and assistance along the way matters.

Understanding that starting in less or more favorable positions isn't something that defines us also matters. Allowing ourselves to see advantages and handicaps for what they are helps us see the world more clearly and more accurately gauge relative capability. It also helps us to see how we might better work with what we have, and augment the efforts of others. To be able to see potential in a person despite their day-to-day struggles is good for all of us. It means more people have the potential to be better utilized, and are more likely to have the chance to reach their full potential. The more humans we have flexing whatever muscles they've got, the more likely we are to have the mental, physical, and observational resources we need to solve the problems we face as a species.

As individuals, this means we take the time to recognize our own privileges and disadvantages. Don't allow these to be crutches or excuses, but recognize them. Pat yourself on the back for overcoming hurdles, and for working hard. Forgive yourself for not yet crossing the finish line in areas where you started further back than others. Remind yourself that you can overcome anything; it may just take a little more effort for you than for some other people.

Don't compare your efforts to those of your peers. Everything you do should be customized for your individual circumstances.

Recognize this in yourself, but also extend the same

courtesy to others. Forgive, encourage, and acknowledge value and effort, even if it doesn't bear the same fruit as it might for someone else. Acknowledge disadvantages where they exist, but don't allow these handicaps to serve as excuses for them not living up to their potential. Celebrate successes even more enthusiastically when the ladder they had to climb was not just taller than for most people, but also missing rungs and on fire.

We should also keep this in mind as we legislate, and as we evolve our approaches to organization and education. In an ideal system, the playing field should be level for everyone. This doesn't mean pulling anyone down, but rather uplifting everyone so they have the same access to fundamentals like food and clean water, electricity and the internet. There should also be access to basic levels of education, a universal expectation of security, and the ability to shape one's own educational experience along the way.

This is feasible. This is something some countries have gotten close to achieving already, though for some of them it's been at the expense of other countries and people, contemporarily or historically.

Spreading these options and opportunities far and wide is still possible, but it will require a reimagining of how we interact with each other, and less focus on stockpiling and building dynasties. It's wonderful that we hope to provide our children with every advantage, but it's better to ensure that everyone, and all their children, have the same.

We can and should aspire to live in a world where advantages are no longer advantages, but merely the default state all people enjoy.

Very Big Things

To a non-scientist, it can be difficult to understand why spending billions of dollars on a particle collider is a good investment.

Okay, sure, it's an impressive machine. And it slams particles together. And we may discover something or whatever. But so what? Couldn't that money be better spent elsewhere?

It seems to be a fundamental property of anything on the fringes of current mainstream understanding that despite often being some of the most vital issues of our time, they're misunderstood, conflated with other issues, or ignored.

Our exploration of particle physics is important because it allows us to understand the structure of the universe. This is a goal that can seem both too big to worry about and too vague to possibly matter to us on the individual level, but it's neither. Doing this research, conducting these experiments, is what lays the groundwork for everything else we do. The electronics age was predicated on this same type of exploration: experiments into conducting materials, heat dissipation, a deeper understanding of electrons, and fabrication at the nano-scale. Without basic research, without fundamental, seemingly boring scientific progress, we wouldn't have any of these things. We wouldn't have much of what we've discovered since the Enlightenment Era, in fact. Lacking boring investments on this scale, we'd probably still be fighting our wars using trebuchets and blunderbusses, and we'd probably still think miasmas or evil spirits cause disease.

The trouble is these very big things we need to understand are not easily discussed, nor intuitively connected to our everyday lives. These realms of study require years of focused education just to get in the door, because the complexity of the issues involved is immense.

Gravity waves, for instance, are ripples in space-time. Not ripples of waves inside the measurable universe like everything else of which we've ever been aware, but ripples in reality, in the space and time in which all those other things exist. This is some heady, far-out stuff, and it requires a completely new way of thinking. This new way of thinking runs perpendicular to the very practical, very isolated perspectives that are trained into us at an early age.

It makes sense we would put on blinders when it comes to these bigger issues, consciously or unconsciously. We have enough to worry about in our concrete, understandable world, thank you very much, and ripples in space-time, when compared to paying rent and pursuing personal fulfillment, don't seem like much of a priority.

While this may be true for actual participation in this research—I'm certainly not qualified to operate a particle accelerator—I would argue an understanding of the basics of these big-picture issues is key, not just to being more aware of what connects to what but also in our capacity to have a better life, and to build something as a species that might set more of us free from the seemingly vital but actually quite small concerns that dominate our thoughts, today.

The development of the atomic bomb was a very real technological feat that changed the world in many ways. It changed the potential of war, it changed the balance of international power, and it changed the thinking of ordinary citizens who both feared and revered its awesome capability.

The atomic bomb is an example of technology derived from fundamental developments in physics. Technology is science made tangible, made practical. We do not get technology without this research. Although the iPhone as a complete product may get all the headlines, the scientific research that allowed for the creation of smaller processors, touchscreens, denser batteries, and wireless connectivity are the real heroes.

When you look at technology, try to see the science that made it possible, and try to understand what other discoveries and developments led to those technologies. Because none of this research, these experiments, happen in isolation. They're all predicated on the work of other scientists and researchers over the years.

Modern computer hardware is based on a device created by Charles Babbage in the 19th century called the Difference Engine. This mechanical device helped solve equations, and led to the development of a more powerful machine, also created by Babbage, called the Analytical Engine. Both devices were spiritual successors to auto-loom technologies, which were used for making textiles at the time. Industrial Revolution-era textile machines could be controlled using punch cards, allowing the manufacturer to essentially code in a pattern using pieces of paper with holes in them. The Analytical Engine supported the use of these cards for mathematical equations, but the real innovation, which led to the development of modern software, was developed by a woman named Ada Lovelace. She realized that these machines were, in effect, programmable. If you could instruct them to crunch numbers, you could, in theory, instruct them to do just about anything. So much of modern society is predicated on the use of software, and it all started with Lovelace and her ideas and research. Every computer we use is a descendent of Babbage's Analytical Engine.

Is it important to know about Babbage and Lovelace in order to make use of the smartphone in your pocket? No.

But does knowing the origins of these technologies allow you to, perhaps, better see how other discoveries and technologies might evolve into what comes next? What replaces smartphones, what contemporary software will become, tomorrow?

Quite possibly. And seeing these connections, these mutations, these ideas made manifest, allows us to better connect cause and effect, and the relationships between disparate-seeming ideas and happenings. Which in turn allows us to make better decisions, which will hopefully make the world a better place.

Many people misunderstand genetically modified foods. When told genetically modified apples will be sold in grocery stores, well-meaning people picket and boycott, demanding these fruits be labeled and sequestered from their pure, clean, natural kin. They post angry missives on Facebook about how they don't want their apples to taste like fish, or to give their children exotic diseases.

There are a few things worth knowing about genetically modified foods that are generally left out of this conversation, both because they're complex issues that most people don't take the time or have the background to understand, and because it serves certain economic interests to obscure the facts.

First, the blending of genetic materials in our food is something that's been going on for ages. Gregor Mendel, an Austrian monk and botanist who bred pea plants in the early

19th century discovered by breeding the right plants in the right way, he could, over time, get bigger, sweeter, greener pea pods. Manipulation of genetics, then, was feasible, even in pre-modern times.

Second, when we genetically manipulate food, we're not doing anything unnatural, we're simply speeding up nature. We don't yet have the ability to hand-code new information into genes, so the idea that we're creating dangerous new species of fruit is a gross misunderstanding of what's happening. We can take existing, natural traits and move them from one genetic strand to another. That means these are traits that already exist: this particular apple family is quite crisp and this one is quite red, and by getting the plants to breed, we could make very crisp, red apples. What happens in the lab is essentially the same thing, it just runs through more offspring, faster, or allows less common traits to be seen in offspring more often. If sweetness is rare, we can make it common and see if that is a favorable trait.

Third, when we move this genetic information from one species to another, this generally grants the recipient abilities that are not often found in its own species, but which are, again, also quite natural. Scientists have been able to make all kinds of animals glow by moving phosphorescent genes from jellyfish into fish and goats and pigs. They've also been able to move a preservative trait from fruit into other fruit, which means that we see an immense reduction in food waste in grocery stores, as the apples will last longer on the shelves before becoming rotten. This is a single line of code from the billions that make up that donor, and much of what's copy-pasted between species is shared information to begin with. This is, again, something that happens in nature all the time, we're just speeding it up and making it more intentional.

Animal genes have not yet been inserted into fruit or vegetables. There's an old piece of anti-GMO propaganda that was disseminated widely announcing fish genes had been transferred into tomatoes. This was believed without question by people who didn't understand the concept of genetic modification science fully enough to understand why this was an unlikely proposition. Could it be done at some point? Almost certainly. Would the process be unnatural? It depends on your definition, but anything moved would be natural, it would just end up in another natural thing. And the tomatoes would not taste like fish, as these propaganda pieces claimed, they might simply be more cold-resistant. How things like taste emerge from genes is another widely misunderstood facet of science.

Finally, it's important to understand that the pushback against a lot of beneficial scientific developments has a financial motivation. The entities who invented terms like 'Frankenfood' to describe genetically modified foods are paid by companies that slap often meaningless terms on their produce, like 'organic,' which is a term that sounds great but is usually unregulated and allows that company to charge more. This mislabeling and preponderance of misinformation causes people who care about what they eat to dismiss the very foods, and innovations in food science, that they would probably be in favor of if they understood the truth. The efforts of these companies to smear GM foods has been one of the larger marketing success stories of recent times, but it's also unfortunate for poorer people and those living in food deserts who might benefit from the increased yields and higher vitamin content of many GM products.

There's a widespread anti-technology, anti-science movement happening around the world right now, and unfortunately that's a statement I could probably make at almost any point in history and it would still be accurate.

Romanticizing a return to nature, doing things the natural, organic way, stepping away from technology, are all responses to fast-moving developments that make us feel stressed and uncomfortable. Things are happening at a pace we can't keep up with, and societal norms, and our own understanding of these movements, have not matched the speed at which tech and science are moving.

As a result, the very things that have added so much enlightenment and luxury to our lives become the focuses of our stress and discontent. Our smartphones are soul-sucking black holes of unhappiness, not omni-tools which make each and every one of us a million times more capable than we are without them. The entertainments we have access to are laziness-inducing brain-drainers, not incredible feats of storytelling and perspective-shifting empathy-exercisers. The foods in our stores are monstrous examples of man's arrogance run amok, not marvels of the modern age, allowing us to enjoy a wide variety of culinary options year-round.

That we're afraid of and complaining about the very things that have liberated us from labor and toil so we have the time to feel afraid and complain is kind of silly. But in the thick of things, without stepping back and establishing that context, and without having a complete understanding of how we achieved and received all these gifts, it's understandable all we'd see are the potential downsides.

And there are downsides, don't get me wrong. The multinational corporation Monsanto is a clear example of what can go wrong when the magic of science and technology meld with some of the more unfortunate developments in corporate law and government. This is a company that, like many companies of its scale and scope, abuses the law and manipulates regulation to favor itself. Although it's developed some truly impressive things by scientific standards, the way it uses these things and the way it competes in the markets it dominates have been anything but broadly beneficial.

Unfortunately, a lot of people conflate all genetically modified foods with companies like Monsanto, and that could not be a more inappropriate connection. Genetically modified crops feed famine-prone areas by allowing the locals to grow several harvests in a single season. They allow malnourished kids to grow up strong and healthy, because their rice now contains vitamins that they would otherwise lack. When we complain about GM foods, we're aiming at the wrong target. We should be targeting the corporate structures that allow for abuse, not the discoveries and developments which help us survive and thrive more equitably, around the world.

The same is true in many industries. Many people are critical of the whole of the pharmaceutical industry, when they should be criticizing individual companies and conglomerates which abuse the system rather than the science that underpins the miracles we've come to expect in the 21st century. What we're capable of today, in every industry and field of inquiry, is the consequence of the health we take for granted. There's room for improvement in any field, of course, but we won't see any positive changes if we broadly and ignorantly accuse entire industries of malpractice, when in reality it's a lumbering few that give all the other players in that space a bad name.

If we're to know who to point the finger at and who to thank and celebrate, we have to understand the fundamentals of very big things. We have to understand particle accelerators, fundamental physics, what GM actually means, and which theories about the structure of the universe are currently most supported by evidence.

It's easy to criticize when we don't take responsibility for understanding that which we're criticizing. The targets are larger and easier to hit. The differences between friend and foe are blurred so that while we may fire our projectiles in the right general direction, we may also sometimes hit the wrong targets.

But if we want to instigate change through our actions, we

should probably make sure we're changing the right things and booting the bad actors, not the science saints and miracle workers.

It's our responsibility, then, to become not just more self-aware, but more deeply informed individuals. This makes it more likely that when we organize as groups, as societies, we'll rally to make beneficial changes and amplify positive efforts.

Maintenance

Janitorial work is difficult work.

It's a job that involves literally cleaning up other people's mess. It's ridding floors of shoe-scum. It's disinfecting handrails. It's cleaning toilets and razoring gooey, half-melted bumper stickers from windows.

The janitors of the world face this maintenance gauntlet daily, coming out the other side alive. Because of janitors, our spaces are cleaner, our environments are reset, and our trash cans are not overflowing with garbage.

The labor involved in maintenance work is laudable. The steadfast repetition of the task, I would argue, is borderline heroic.

This is the nature of infrastructural tasks. They are more predictable than the edgy, fringy work of inventing new things or interacting with people. They require sturdiness and resolve because they're so tedious, not because they're steeped in the unexpected. They're monumentally under-appreciated, often reckoned near the bottom of the hierarchy, which is fitting only in the sense that they do, in fact, provide a solid foundation for all the other work we do as a species.

I've lived in cities where trash fills the streets and the toilets are never cleaned. It's not pleasant, and it's not a fully operational environment. Having your trash remain uncollected is a seemingly minor inconvenience, but if it sits there long enough, after a while it becomes clear rather quickly why systems of trash collection are as integral as they are. The rot, the microorganisms, the smell, the space occupied by the growing, squishy mass of discarded matter. When we can safely ignore this aspect of our lives, can just toss things in the proper bins and forget about them, we're more capable of focusing, of committing ourselves to the work we're undertaking. When that pile of detritus is never out of sight, however, it's a very different situation. The realities of a disorderly real world creep into our consciousness and prevent us from completely extracting ourselves from earthly concerns.

The mythos of the heroic individual has come to dominate international pop culture. And though there are still competing ideologies, much of the world's technology and business culture is shaped by the "great man" theory of innovation. We see capable rebels who're willing to knock over tables and shout loudly as the most likely bringers of change. These people with this personality type, then, have become the most celebrated. We love legends of brilliant and flawed heroes. We love looking back at their lives and romanticizing everything, pulling quotes from innocuous sentences and telling stories that seem to support whatever point we want to make in the moment.

This mythology is, of course, sometimes based on fact. There are many innovations and breakthroughs that have been made by an individual: by a rogue scientist, by a rude but insightful middle manager, by an upstart entrepreneur who wouldn't take no for an answer.

But these tales are almost always not the whole story. Even these "great men" require janitors and trash collectors and construction workers and electricians to operate optimally. A lot of innovation, creation, and even disruption in every industry are not attributable to a single person or small group of people, but rather the consequence of persistent iteration over time. It's the result not of a eureka moment, but of a slow, unsexy, plodding sequence of tasks completed by people who probably aren't being paid enough, and who themselves wouldn't necessarily consider the work they do to be terribly important beyond it allowing them to pay the bills.

We know this to be true, on some level. There are not enough mythologized figures in the world to account for even the most obvious innovations, not to mention all the invisible luxuries, like the aforementioned trash-free streets and sidewalks.

But we're fed a steady stream of Hercules and Rambo tales as children, and in these stories, it's seldom the humble paycheck-earner working from a cubicle who saves the day. It's that singular, bulletproof warrior who plows through lesser humans to achieve something grand. This is such a common trope that we even have a name and template for it, developed by the American scholar Joseph Campbell in his book *The Hero with a Thousand Faces*. He calls this journey the monomyth, and summarizes it as such:

"A hero ventures forth from the world of common day into a region of supernatural wonder. Fabulous forces are there encountered and a decisive victory is won. The hero comes back from this mysterious adventure with the power to bestow boons on his fellow man."

The monomyth starts with our hero, uneasy with the default state of things, shown against the backdrop of a contemporary moment in time. He receives a call to adventure, refuses the call, and then meets with a mentor who helps him on the journey. The hero then crosses the threshold into this new world, a wider world he never would have seen or experienced had he stayed within the status quo. There is then a series of tests, encounters with new allies, a confrontation with death or destruction, a reward of some kind for overcoming this hurdle, a return to his previous home, the real world outside of his adventure, and then one more monumental test, which purifies the hero, and elevates him to a higher level. The hero then "returns with the elixir," essentially bringing back whatever he's won, whatever he's learned, to the common person.

This archetypical hero's journey is remarkably common in the stories we tell our children and ourselves. From the oldest creation myths propagated only through oral histories, to the newest Pixar films, we see the same processes played out over and over again, almost without fail.

There is, of course, nothing inherently wrong with this. But one weakness of the hero's journey mythology is that it leads us to believe we're all going to be heroes, we're all going to be famous, we're all going to be president, and if not, what's the point? What value can we possibly have as a lesser human being? As such, doesn't it make sense to fight tooth-and-claw, to even do things that might be morally corrupt to get where we want to be? To be the hero of the tale?

If it's foretold in the stars, if we're destined to do great things, wouldn't any sacrifice, any breach of decorum, be prudent to reach those goals?

It's useful to view the misbehavior of public figures through this lens. If a politician sees herself as the hero of her own story, why wouldn't she manipulate the system in a misleading or illegal way to achieve what she's been promised by this belief system? By this logic, all her flubs and failures, her mistakes and misdeeds, will someday be rewritten as part of her noble journey.

Massive character flaws are often reframed as assets by historians and biographers because it's assumed being a prick or abusing their spouse was just part of what made a remarkable person so remarkable. It made them a rounder, larger-than-life character. It would weaken the story to have a hero who's actually a villain, rather than a hero who misbehaves because he's a very special rule breaker.

The tale of a horrible person who chances upon a useful innovation is not a biography many people would want to buy, nor is it a story that would be told and retold at tech conferences.

Which brings us back to the invisibility of the maintainers in our collective mythology. These are the people in the stories who help the hero get where he needs to go. They represent the innocent townspeople, or the ignorant villager who needs to be shown right from wrong by the hero. They're in the background, largely unmentioned, but who maintains the treacherous road leading through the mountain to the oracle's hut? It sure as hell isn't the oracle, and the hero never thinks to comment on it. There's a decent chance had this path not been carved, and had it not been kept clear of rubble, the hero never would have made it to the oracle in the first place, and would never have learned of her fantastic destiny.

What we choose to celebrate informs how we act and what behavior we reward. Am I saying we need to hold a parade for every individual who works in city maintenance? No. But would it be a nice gesture to have a day of appreciation and recognition for city workers as a group? I think so, yes. I also think it would help us remember these massive, complex structures we built, both physical and societal, require the effort of many not just the one or two people whose faces we regularly see on television. We use individuals as stand-ins for the whole, but they are not the whole and it's inappropriate to treat them as if they are.

We should ask ourselves how we might better align our

system of rewards so there's more incentive to happily dedicate oneself to maintenance tasks, rather than trying to be the next celebrity or superstar CEO. Almost all of the incentives fall heavily in favor of the hero, not the other characters in the story, which seems to indicate we need to be telling a different story. Maybe a riff on the old model, but one which allows us to feel good about slow iteration and regular upkeep, rather than just blowing up old ideas and ignoring the rubble, leaving it for someone else, some unnamed character, to deal with.

Many of the marvels of the modern world are the result of systems that allow us to work together, rather than one invention or innovation. These systems have also evolved, little by little, branching out into a vast array of different approaches and specialties, serving different locations, groups of people, and purposes.

Systems do not function in isolation. Systems are not maintained by a hero at a central terminal. Systems allow us to orchestrate complex routines and tasks so our garbage collectors' efforts synchronize with those of the janitors, while the electricians' work allows us to benefit from that of the construction workers who erected a new electrical substation down the street.

Not every societal change requires legislative action or official decree. We, the individual nodes of our society, can decide to place more emphasis on the maintenance, on the maintainers. Not to instill a new imbalance away from the individual, romanticizing the collective, but to establish a better balance between the two. Each of us could be seen as a hero, playing our role alongside other heroes, doing heroic things like keeping the lights on and trash off the streets.

Maybe sometimes we step outside the network, break things, and build something unprecedented. But most of the time, we are one part of a larger heroic system. We're an integral part of an ever-evolving society that doesn't collapse with every shift and revolutionary idea. We're building and maintaining an environment in which we can feel confident in our ability to make things better: secure in our assiduously maintained safety and stability, and consequently comfortable with the idea of change.

Resilience

Being resilient means different things at distinct times. It also differs based on whether we're discussing societies or individuals, and the environment in which we find ourselves.

Resilience is a word that actually straddles two sometimes oppositional ideas but blends them into one.

One definition is related to the ability to survive and sustain. Resiliency is what allows us to face difficulties and survive them, standing back up and moving forward when everything else around us has been blasted to rubble.

The other definition is more about flexibility. A resilient material is bendy, pliable, and able to be warped wildly before popping back to its original form. You can crush it, tie it in a knot, pull it till it seems likely to break, and yet it will always spring back, no worse for the wear.

I love this blend of ideas. We often think of surviving as being sturdy and steadfast, as rugged and maybe a little bulky. Tanks are meant to plow right through the center of things and absorb damage that would obliterate a human being, and they've become so well known for this property that "tank" has become an adjective. Calling someone a tank of a person means they're not going down with just one punch.

But resiliency implies there's a different way to approach survival than sheer sturdiness. We needn't be the strongest, the most dense or armored. We needn't be the most ferocious or cunning, either. We simply need to be capable of bending when it makes sense to bend, and then, just as importantly, capable of springing back into shape.

There's no good military metaphor for this, but there is an evolutionary one: human beings.

Our ancestors were not exactly the most impressive specimens when it came to tooth-, claw-, and muscle-based combat. We could scurry back into the trees for a time, and after we started walking upright, we could watch for predators moving through the tall grass and hide ourselves, maybe occasionally scaring them off, though with mixed results.

But we were good at moving and working together, using a kind of pack-hunting instinct that later evolved into tribalism. We could signal each other and plan out attacks, which was something most other creatures could not do. And particularly in the truly primeval moments of our species' past, a lot of what we hunted or fended off were big frickin' monsters the size of minivans or long-haul trucks that, by any estimate, would have the upper hand in these confrontations.

In most ways, of course, they did. They were the tanks. They were beasts built to survive and sustain. They were alpha creatures at the top of the food chain.

They had bulk, they had inbuilt weaponry, they had evolutionary places of honor. But they didn't have resilience. They were so specialized, so unyielding, that as change occurred in the environment and in the creatures around them, they failed to keep up. Their very strength and physical durability proved a burden rather than a boon when it became more beneficial to require less energy, to need less food, and to be capable of moving into more diverse ecological niches rather than sitting at the tippy-top of just a few limited food webs.

Our species survived pre-history because of our ability to warp and reshape ourselves whilst still maintaining the fundamentals of who we are. We've set up shop in every environmental extreme, and weathered the worst nature has to offer. We've stepped into the territories of countless nightmarish beasts, only to come out on top. Not because we could beat them directly in feats of strength, but because we could outwit them, out-survive them, out-collaborate them. We learned to fend off polar bears and survive in extreme arctic temperatures. We learned to live alongside tigers and survive irregular, catastrophic droughts and floods. Our species has somehow survived and thrived in Australia, even though every venomous monster that lives there wants to kill us and the vast majority of the continent is desert.

We've done well. We've overcome a lot. And in the coming years, we'll need to continue to do so.

What we face now are many and varied new realities, some of which are the consequences of our own actions. The climate is changing, and we haven't seen anywhere near the worst of it yet. Even if you're one of the few who thinks this has less to do with human activity and more to do with the natural processes catching up with us, we still have a lot of changes ahead, and a lot of decisions to make.

For instance: how do we disseminate information to people who believe such wildly different things? How do we organize action on the scale of billions?

In the case of global climate change, what we face isn't a "global warming," a term that has been phased out because it never accurately described what's happening around the world. Instead what we'll see, and are already seeing, is a rewiring of how planetary systems operate, and a resultant amplification of extremes.

Our trade winds and ocean currents have already started

changing direction, and they may in some places disappear entirely. These channels are what allow us to safely travel via ship and plane, making use of reliable historical data to keep us from, say, stumbling into immensely high- or low-pressure zones that could knock our 747 out of the sky, or find ourselves fighting ocean currents that force us to use twice as much fuel to get where we're going.

Beyond travel, these circulatory elements are key components of the water cycle and of our weather systems. The trade winds are the result of high- and low-pressure systems which regulate temperature, carry seeds and spores between landmasses, enable migratory patterns in birds and other animals, and maintain many natural systems we've come to rely on across the generations.

The currents in the ocean are the result of warming and cooling, and the salinization and desalination of water. Water of different temperatures and compositions move up and down, which cycles the material we find at each depth. This causes biomass from the bottom of the ocean to move to the top, feeding the microorganisms which live there, which in turn are fed upon by larger and larger creatures in the food web. The biomass originates with the sun, which is photosynthesized by phytoplankton, which then die, fall to the bottom, and become biomass which is eventually pulled back up by that water churn.

If this system is altered by a change in density resulting from a change in the salinity of the water, which in turn changes the buoyancy of the water at different stratification levels, then we have an upset food web, which can collapse, sometimes slowly, sometimes quite quickly. Since one billion people are directly dependent on the ocean for food, this is a human issue, not just an ecological one.

The impact this has on our winds and ocean currents doesn't stop with the biology of those ecosystems. When these systems change, so does the weather. We've already begun to see some of the consequences of minor shifts to these systems, in the record-high temperatures in the Northern Hemisphere and record lows in parts of the Southern Hemisphere. The ice in the Arctic is melting, and looks likely to disappear completely within a few decades at the high end of estimates. There have been tornadoes in Los Angeles, once-every-thousand-years-strength hurricanes happening three times in as many years, and flooding both inland and on the coast. The maps showing which coastlines will be underwater with even a moderate oceanic rise—just two inches—are humbling. Many of humanity's largest, most populated and historically significant cities would be underwater. And two inches is well below the rise that's being predicted for the next decade by even the most conservative climate scientists. There's a possibility these changes could occur even sooner, which would restrict our chances of building proper dykes, walls, and pumps quickly enough, before the water rise becomes critical.

I'm not painting this picture to convince you we're all going to die and everything sucks. I want to present some of the issues we face to illustrate that, although the situation is in many ways dire, it's also not insurmountable. We are an immensely resilient species, and though that doesn't always mean we're the strongest or the most tank-like, it does mean we're skilled adjusters and adapters.

There's little chance, at this point, we'll be able to stave off all the negative impacts of climate change. It is a cyclical process that was bound to happen eventually, and though we've sped it forward by hundreds or thousands of years, and as a result been caught largely unprepared for what's happened and what's coming next, I still believe we're more than capable of handling the challenges we're going to collectively face.

If we want to not just survive, but thrive, however, we're

going to need to tap deep into our intellectual reserves and come up with better ways to work together. The tools we have now are not up to snuff for the battles we're going to fight and need to win. Our inability to agree on what's happening with the climate is an indication of the strength of our global system, I would argue, because it means we're capable of seeing multiple sides of the same issue and of having a discussion about it. The weakness, though, is our inability to act as quickly as we need to act on critical matters, and to come up with plans that are actionable, even when we can't agree on the complete outline or specifics of the situation we face.

We've created a system with incentives that are misaligned with where we're going and where we need to be. We reward traits that serve us well under normal, predictable circumstances, but which are often insufficient for situations in which risks need to be taken and decisive action is required. Incorruptible, ideological politicians do still rise through the ranks sometimes, but they tend to be the exception, not the rule, and much of the real power rests in the hands of cowards and influence-grabbers rather than people who are capable of making smart choices for the whole, even when they conflict with their personal interests.

Our continued resilience, then, is not just dependent on our creation of clever technological and sociological solutions to the immediate dangers we face. It's not just about figuring out ways to pollute less and create clean energy, to reimagine urban centers and come up with efficient desalination processes. We need to rework and rebuild our systems so we focus on our resiliency, rather than pure, tank-like strength. We've been through an era in which military and economic might have been among the most important attributes for a society because we had stable footing in most other regards. But that footing has been lost, and we're prone to fall unless we reallocate our efforts—and that means the efforts of our states, of our elected officials, of our meta-national corporations—toward the new issues of the day. Toward, essentially, figuring out what the future of everything will look like when the world around us has changed dramatically, away from the world in which we came to be, and came of age.

We can weather this storm. We can stand back up after we get knocked down. But what will we find when we do?

Will our cities remain, husks of what they once were, flooded at ground-level but survivable up top, the wealthy and influential having bulwarked themselves against the worst of the changes but also having kept things largely as they were, old power structures in place though worse for the wear? Or will we find we've bent in the wind, reshaped with the environment, created novel ways of living, new ways of interacting, innovative methods of organizing and ruling and deliberating, better means of sharing information and acting upon it, and improved definitions of success, stature, and strength?

Turning points of this kind are not unique. On a historical scale, this has happened before. And though the challenge is different each time, as are the people being asked to bend for the betterment of all, it's still a task we've proven ourselves equal to every time. Our species wouldn't still be alive and growing if that weren't the case.

We have every reason to believe the same is true today, that we're equal to this challenge, no matter how remote that possibility might seem on the ground level. We as a species have shown ourselves to be remarkably capable of reimagining how things could be, changing ourselves and changing the world around us to make those visions manifest.

We as individuals have to be open to change and embrace our capacity to bend before our societies will. If we can come to see malleability as a strength rather than a weakness, and allow that ideology to seep into how we interact and organize, we'll be in a very good position to roll with any challenges we face.

Data & Technology

We're undergoing a dramatic shift in how we organize, work, interact, and think.

There are many issues that contribute to this rising tide, the beginnings of which you can already see, if you look around. There are social changes occurring alongside economic ones. We have different expectations, as groups of people and as individuals, than we've ever had in the past. We're more empowered as a consequence of choices and efforts made by those who came before us.

But few things will have the same staggering impact as the technologies that are coming of age today, and which will continue to change us in the coming years.

Though perhaps I should say, "The technologies we will use to change ourselves," because it wouldn't be correct to anthropomorphize these systems and this hardware. They are remarkable tools, yes, but not capable of having their own wants and needs. They require drivers, and we are the only creatures capable of getting behind the wheel.

Technology has empowered us since our earliest days of existence. Simple tools, made from wood, then stone, allowed our ancestors to out-perform other hunting and gathering creatures in our environment. We evolved alongside our tools, and those who were the most capable of inventing, building, and using them were the most likely to survive. We're all the descendants of Stone Age da Vincis.

Those simple innovations—spears, bows and arrows, carving tools, fire-making tools, clothing—carried us through tens of thousands of years of development. We eventually learned to work metal, and then to smelt it. After a few thousand more years of whacking each other with more sophisticated, sharper weapons and clothing ourselves in armor made of reshaped, refined minerals, we aimed our intellects at something more complex.

Machines were inventions made up of many smaller inventions, all of which worked in synchronization to accomplish something larger and more complex. Sprockets and springs were inventions that, when working together, had far more utility than in isolation.

Machines were originally developed in simple and complex forms in cultures around the world. Some of the earliest were born in the Eastern world, in China, and what we would today call the Middle East, but were often seen as interesting novelties and toys for the wealthy, rather than as a worthwhile intellectual endeavor. Complex machines arrived early in these cultures, but were not taken seriously, or applied widely beyond entertainment.

Circumstances were different in the Western world, where the populations were, on average, not as developed, but which underwent a Renaissance at a fortuitous time in history, with favorable trade routes, a complimentary climate, and a slew of new inventions having recently arrived from around the world, their innovations noted, studied, reworked, and built-upon. This stage of technological development lasted a few hundred years, which seems like a long time by today's standards, but was in that era the speediest period of innovation ever documented.

Then came the next, even more abbreviated period.

The Industrial Revolution is a label loosely applied to a collection of decades between the years 1760 and 1830 AD. Over the course of less than a century, the human race, and particularly those living in Europe and its sub-regions, saw more technological and infrastructural change in a single lifetime than any generation in history.

This shift was the result of innovations that allowed for the mechanization of production. Rather than simply being able to create clever weapons or interesting toys using mechanical pieces, we were now able to create many things mechanically.

One of the first industries to mechanize was the textile industry, a major source of wealth for the region, and a field which was existentially threatened by cheap textiles arriving from India. Textile work at the time was immensely labor intensive, and required a great deal of time and effort to produce a single garment, a single sheet for a bed, a single set of curtains. Inventions like the cotton gin, which inexpensively helped remove seeds from raw cotton, and the spinning mule, which was a machine that helped refine now-seedless cotton into high-quality thread, incrementally reduced the amount of time and labor required, while also increasing the quality of the end product. Eventually, these and other innovations were strung together into textile manufacturing processes, and when combined with organizational systems of labor— bringing all these machines and their operators to one location so they could work together as a larger system—the amount of product created by each laborer was increased by a factor of 40, and their quality far outshone that which was arriving from India.

The benefits of industrializing the textile industry were immense and multifaceted. Those who worked in the industry were able to make more money, and the industry could support more laborers, as there was more product to sell. Exports increased, as did the reputation of the regional industry. This further increased demand, which allowed for more expansion and development of these systems, which increased the effectiveness and efficiency of the work being done.

This boom wasn't limited to textiles. It extended to chemicals, cement, glass, agricultural products, food, mining and metallurgy, and eventually, machine tools and steam power.

Beyond the immense productivity gains and wealth brought to the area as a result of this shift, society changed dramatically, as well. Women were suddenly able to work outside the home, with other women in textile factories. This changed their interpersonal social dynamics, their role in the economy, and their family lives.

Just as with textiles, agricultural production increased, meaning farmers could produce more food per plot of land, which sparked a population boom. Infrastructure was built and refined, leading to more and better roads and railways, which fueled the growing desire for information about the region and about the world and allowed more people to travel greater distances than ever before. Standards of living increased across the board, and systems of government, which were mostly monarchal or other flavors of totalitarianism at the time, were questioned, and in some cases augmented or replaced by newly powerful businesspeople and a burgeoning middle class. Citizenry were suddenly able to afford things and live beyond mere subsistence. They were able to think about their place in the world, not just how they'd put food on the table that day.

The evolution of machines and technology is what liberated us from spending all our time and energy, throughout our entire lives, ensuring we have just enough to get by and maybe to reproduce.

The human story of the 200 years since the Industrial Revolution has, in a lot of ways, been a story of technology. The setting, the social standards, our very way of life, have been defined by the technologies that have emerged and changed things from generation to generation, and increasingly midway through generations. In the 21st century, it's unlikely any age demographic will make it from birth to death without seeing at least a few major breakthroughs, which result in massive culture shifts and readjustments of power. Imagine the change someone born during the Great Depression in the early 1930s would have seen in their lifetime, had they lived till 2017.

People born today have even more change than their predecessors to look forward to; or viewed another way, to cope with. Because these changes aren't necessarily good or wholesome, not beneficial to all, or even beneficial at all. We have achieved fundamental human rights for a huge chunk of the human population alive today, but they are not equally disseminated, and not available to all. These rights are also not seen as universally positive changes to everyone. The changing dynamics of family life, which provided women with more social standing, power, and options, are regarded by some to have caused a truly negative societal shift.

We develop our technologies and we also decide how to use them. It's possible to build a steam engine and to use it only for war and death and destruction. It's also possible to use it to unshackle those who were previously tied to the land against their will, and vastly increase the potential of every human being.

The value of each of these changes is subjective, but we can adjust the course of the landslides triggered when new technologies are introduced. You can't put the genie back into the bottle, but you can wish for things you believe will serve humanity well, rather than for things that will reinforce existing, flawed structures against change.

Charles Babbage saw potential in textile machines which used punch-cards to tell the machine to produce specific patterns, and built computing machines that utilized this input mechanism. Ada Lovelace took things a step further by recognizing that Babbage's machine could be used for purposes beyond just math, which led to her becoming the world's first computer programmer and the developer of the very first computer algorithm. These were both vital step for humanity, as much of our modern technology is based upon programmed computers and the algorithms they run.

The microchip was another fundamental piece of modern technological infrastructure, as it allowed us to build, and then quickly iterate, increasingly powerful machines to work on increasingly sophisticated problems.

Most early computers worked like the mechanical contraptions built in Lovelace's day, but the physical logic gates that would be opened and closed were replaced by electronic logic gates, non-tangible ones and zeroes. The modern computer, then, looks a lot different than one from the Industrial Revolution, but operates according to many of the same theories. The programming languages used today are several levels higher in sophistication than anything used back in the early days of the microchip, which means more of the fundamental processes have been made simple and intuitive. Due to these improvements in hardware and in software, the modern programmer, and everyday computer user, wields far more power than those of previous generations.

Just as inventions were combined with other inventions to make more complex machinery, our modern, non-tangible inventions are bundled with more of the same to create something larger and more powerful. Our software has been systematized, as programs are blended with other programs to create bigger, more sophisticated programs.

Understanding the historical significance of our technology is vital if we're going to make informed choices about what's happening in the world today. Our powers have increased, societal evolution is inextricably linked to our technological development, and the average person has more power to create and destroy than ever before.

Big Data is powered by algorithms that crunch millions of data points together, then extracts from that information completely new data points, original observations, and novel connections we likely wouldn't or couldn't have noticed. Our capacity for working with information is flexible, but on massive scales our abilities are very limited. Machines are filling in those gaps for us, though as with any new capability, Big Data represents both promise and peril, depending on how we use it.

We're developing increasingly sophisticated artificial intelligence (AI) software that, although not true intelligence, is still capable of seeing and understanding the world in a limited fashion, and in a different way from humans. This field is progressing with remarkable speed, and a huge portion of our economic, research, and technological infrastructure is already dependent on these AIs.

Is it possible to build sufficient systems, enough infrastructure that's largely self-operating and self-maintaining, that we humans won't be necessary anymore? And if so, what happens to society? What changes can we expect? What will the economy look like when we don't need to work anymore, and couldn't find a job even if we wanted to?

The precipice at which we stand overlooks a vast array of complex systems and fast-moving changes, and it's natural to become frustrated and confused by them. No single person can keep track of everything that's happening and all the powers we now possess, much less make full use of these powers and take complete responsibility for what happens as a consequence of our using them.

But we can, each of us, be aware enough to see the ripples caused by each new development, to imagine the potential they represent, for good and for bad, and to make changes to our own perspectives as a result of that insight. We can also prime our communities to be ready, and to make choices that allow more people to benefit from these evolutions, rather than allowing them to reinforce the status quo and increase preexisting biases, divides, and injustices.

Technologies are tools, and the benefit or burden of tools is dependent on the desires and capabilities of their users. If we can become the people we need to be to use the tools we have today, responsibly, I think we'll find ourselves in a much better place tomorrow. We'll be more than capable of building an increasingly better world for those who come after us.

How We Fight

There's never been a more peaceful time for humans on Earth.

By every relevant metric, including number of conflicts, number of deaths during these conflicts, and even violent crimes in non-war settings, the 21st century, thus far, has been the least violent period in recorded history.

This is not to say there isn't still violence in the world. People are still murdered, rapists still walk the streets, and wars are still declared, or in some cases fought but not declared. There are regions in the world where you wouldn't necessarily see the difference between the status of the locals today and how they fared hundreds of years ago during particularly violent times.

Like technology and other resources, well-being and peace are not uniformly distributed.

But on average, on scale, the trajectory is good. From World War II onward in particular, the decades have been progressively less deadly, and much of the world has been able to use this increase in peace to achieve relative prosperity.

In periods like this one, which we hope will continue, but

which could, of course, prove to be the silence before the storm, it's a good idea to take stock and identify what has worked and what hasn't. To figure out what it is that's allowed us to interact with other nations and with our neighbors in comparable safety, while the same wouldn't have been possible in the past. What's changed? Has the world shifted, or have we?

It's a safe bet the consequences of World War I and World War II played a significant role in the establishment of our current global stability. Again, the rewards were not uniformly distributed, but those who won were largely liberal democracies, and consequently, the world powers in the years since have been progressive and open. There are still authoritarians in the world, and there are even emerging powers, like China, that are further on that side of the spectrum than most governments today. But by and large those who control the world are elected officials, not monarchs or dictators, and that has led to societal growth and economic liberty. Power and wealth have become more distributed, and though there is still a vast gulf between the haves and have-nots, the distance between the two sides is less evident and imposing than during prior generations.

Data shows that democracies are more likely to respect each other's borders, in part, at least, because it's more difficult for hawkish politicians and generals to sell the public on the idea of going to war with other democracies. Authoritarian regimes, yes, and rebel leaders, certainly, but other "civilized" nations? Other groups of free or mostly free people? It's a tough argument to make, and if it's not made convincingly, those in charge are out of a job. The reallocation of this kind of power, then, has made conflict far less likely and has ensured there's almost always less to gain.

That latter point is reinforced by the economic benefits of a world filled with interconnected, globalized nations, connected by trade agreements and international laws to which all but the most fringe nations adhere and contribute. There are many flaws to be found in organizations like the United Nations and World Trade Organization, but it's difficult to dispute that they've made the world a more interconnected place. When the governments and markets of the world are intertwined, international trade becomes immensely profitable, and the consequences of war become a lot more dispersed.

The deck is stacked in favor of this sort of system, post-WWII, which is good because it does make the traditional boots-on-the-ground, bullets-in-the-air type of warfare nearly obsolete.

There are negative consequences to this shift, however. We're finding new and interesting ways to fight, both physically and intangibly, but these novel forms of combat remain untested over long durations and in many cases are completely unregulated, both nationally and internationally.

What this means is that, although we're unlikely to see another World War II-type conflict, we are increasingly likely to see the sort of operation that has decimated Syria. Proxy groups in the country supported in various ways by outside interests with beefs to settle, like the United States and Russia. Rebels and dictators are pitted against one another, with bombing raids and illegal weaponry used against those stuck in the middle. The result is that, as part of what amounts to a large-scale pissing contest between dominant political interests, an entire nation full of people have been uprooted and attacked, their families scattered, their homes demolished, their numbers rapidly diminishing.

Again, conflict on this scale worldwide has nearly disappeared, and used to be a lot more common. But although these incidents are today more regionally contained and strategic, and typically less about conquest than geopolitics or ideology, I'm guessing the high-level details are of little consequence to the people who have lost limbs, loved ones, and lives in devastated cities like Aleppo.

Another type of aggression that's become more prominent was formerly the stuff of spy flicks, but has now become a common front in the shadow-battles between rival governments around the world.

Hacking is an appealing covert military option because it allows one nation to steal from, spy on, and even attack the infrastructure of another nation, and to do so with relative impunity. A hack can be instigated, perhaps even on a massive scale, but available evidence will be unlikely to paint a clear, 100% certain picture of who the perpetrator was. The victim government or other entity, then, will be unable to make a strong public case that they have been attacked by a specific rival, and as such will be unlikely to take any real action, except perhaps a counter-hack, in retaliation.

The trend, then, is away from hands-on, soldiers and tanks-style warfare, and toward more impersonal and indirect head-strikes and body blows. Why send in a hundred soldiers when you can provide weaponry to a local faction of rebels, instead? Why bomb a power plant when you can hack it and achieve some of the same ends while leaving no actionable fingerprints?

Drone strikes are another increasingly common means of divvying out violence, especially from developed nations into those that are less developed. Drones allow soldiers a thousand miles away to launch sorties into enemy territories, taking out specific targets or large groups of people, and without the chance of losing a friendly soldier as a result. Drones are also increasingly automated, so remote soldiers are still politically prudent, but not absolutely necessary to complete a mission. This is particularly true of missions that involve spying rather than bomb-dropping.

Drone strikes are worrying, as they allow one nation to attack another without setting foot in their territory, and without any risk of loss of life on their side. This makes it an easier sell in democratic countries, which means it's an option more likely to be used frequently, and perhaps in situations where other methods would be preferable. When drone killings become the default option for solving problems, antagonism can escalate quickly. Especially when we reach the point where the same type of attack is feasible in return, this will be bad news, not just for soldiers on the ground, but also for civilian populations worldwide who will become tempting and reachable targets.

Beyond the physical, military- and espionage-related conflicts, we're also seeing an amplification of intellectual warfare. The advent of the internet, and the world wide web built atop it, birthed a huge number of communication tools which came of age in a very short time. Within decades we've become an internet technology-reliant species, with huge swathes of our formerly disseminated infrastructure now based in server farms distributed around the world. Much of how we now get our news, look up information, interact with each other, and share resources, is internet-based. And that means the net is a somewhat fragile choke-point, and also a well that's easy to poison. One needn't knock out the internet to render those who depend on it vulnerable. One only need learn to master online tools, or discover the weaknesses of these platforms, and exploit them.

The Russians have been teaching the world a masterclass on the use of these tools to amplify outward-facing propaganda. As a crypto-authoritarian state that goes through the motions of democracy but is in fact ruled by one man, it's important for Vladimir Putin and his inner circle that not only the Russian people, but also a chunk of the wider world believes one particular set of facts. Whether these facts are actually true is irrelevant. By making use of social networks and search results, by manipulating algorithms and hiring professional trolls to muck up the conversation and play with our subconscious herd mentality, he's been able to use the tools and ideals of democracy—that is, representation for all sides of an argument, and communication tools which keep us informed of dissenting opinions—against us.

It's clever, it's devious, and it's effective.

If you can control facts, can make people believe in a particular storyline, then you can also control their actions and even their thoughts. We don't need mind control devices to sway a free and democratic public, we just need plausible stories repeated over and over again, the perception of these stories aligning with our existing beliefs. It also doesn't hurt to have an implied conflict between one group and another traditionally opposing group. By painting a picture using these methods, it's possible to hijack a political party, an election, and most frighteningly, an electorate. An entire chunk of a voting population can be convinced to manipulate their system for you, in your favor. They can be convinced to defend those actions, perhaps even physically, because it's their legal, democratic right to participate and vote however they please. Even if their opinions and beliefs have been hijacked by a steady stream of misinformation and faux facts.

I say this is a lesson because it should remind us that, if we're able to use these same tools, these same communication channels, as well as Russia has, but to convey real information rather than intentionally muddled, slanted propaganda, we stand a good chance of building something stronger than that with which we started. These channels of attack are only effective because the channels themselves are so powerful, but have been long ignored or underutilized by those with valuable information to share.

It's unfortunate we've had to be shown the value of

communication and the potency of our tools by an outside group using them against us. But if we choose to learn this lesson and can survive the consequences of that initial education, we'll find ourselves armed with a powerful barrier against negative intellectual influences in the future.

Note that this doesn't mean we'll prevent dissent or unpopular opinions or arguments from any group that believes differently from us. Those are necessary and valuable aspects of a democracy, and need to be empowered. What we'll prevent is the believable distortion of facts, and the building up of an equivalency in some people's minds between things like science and hoax, progress and being un-American, immigrant and terrorist. The meaning of words and the understanding of our national ideals should not be on the table. We need to be open to change, but that doesn't mean denying reality. It's possible to engage in vital civil discussion and debate without each election representing a possible end to the democratic values and freedoms that serve as the foundation for everything we do.

The battles we choose to fight say something about who we are as people. How we choose to fight these battles also matters.

It may be that drone strikes and hacking prove to be solutions which pull us still further back from the brink of future world wars, and by facing the new dangers and risks they pose, we're actually decreasing the overall level of danger and violence in the world. It may also be the opposite, that these new methods of attack prove to be unregulated hotbeds for terrible acts of aggression, and those who make use of them will need to undergo a serious gut-check and determine if the benefits outweigh the existing and potential consequences.

This is a question we, as individuals, will have to ask ourselves first, as it's unlikely our governments will start that process, sociopathic as they can sometimes be as a result of their very structure. Committees allow individuals to belay their guilt to a larger, unfeeling institution, and that very much includes governmental committees. At the end of the day, the buck stops with us, the citizenry. Whether or not we're the ones giving the orders and controlling the drones, our names are on those missiles, and our inaction implicates us alongside whatever robot consciousness is doing the actual killing.

If we can determine what kind of conflict is necessary to prevent even larger, more violent conflicts, we can build institutions capable of ethically managing such fights, and which will hopefully be capable of recognizing when direct conflict is necessary and when another solution will better serve the interests of not just our individual nations, but of humanity as a whole.

The sooner we start thinking globally, as a planet-spanning species, rather than as isolated warrens of very different creatures, the sooner we'll be able to do away with physical conflict entirely, instead spending our valuable time, energy, and resources on productivity and progress.

Difficult Conversations

There's a difficult conversation occurring in the realm of brain science right now. It's not difficult in the sense that we don't know how to proceed or lack sufficient data to do so; everything in the realm of brain research is still fuzzy so that wouldn't be particularly remarkable.

The difficulty revolves around the issue of race and genetic predisposition, and particularly how it impacts the development of the brain.

There is rightly, I think, trepidation amongst those who do such research, because there is a truly dark history of racial segmentation within many scientific specialties. In recent times, research into genetic differences between genotypes was used to justify the dehumanization of some races while encouraging the favoritism of others. One hundred fifty years ago we still felt legally justified, in part because of scientific findings about the differences between those of African descent and those whose families came from Europe, to enslave the former while the latter became the template of correct, civilized humanity.

This science, as it turned out, was false. There were some who truly believed its voracity, I'm sure, but the processes used to acquire this supposedly legitimate information, and the theories upon which it was based was not up to the standards of modern scientific inquiry. Further, a lot of the research was heavily politicized, and clearly favored the prejudices of the people doing the "research." It was a whole lot of justification without much substance.

A belief in racial genetic hierarchy didn't end there. It continued until the mid- to late-20th century, and still holds weight among some people today, strangely. Even with all the lived experience and scientific data we've accumulated in the meantime, there are still those who cleave to antique beliefs that support their biases.

And this, as much as anything else, is why there's so much discomfort surrounding research that touches on race, racial identity, genetic differences between races, and the like.

Contemporary people still wear societal scars which remind us how bad things can get when data is misunderstood or misused by influential individuals or groups. There's plenty of reason to be suspicious of the motives of those who wish to look into the differences in the rate of brain development between, say, people from Sierra Leone and people who grew up in Arizona. We could learn a lot from such research. It might help us shine light on how a person's access to different types of economic infrastructure, as well as the very small variations in genetic lineage, impact the pace of growth of neural development and overall cognitive capability. Go back far enough and we're all related, but the mutations that have occurred in different groups around the world are real, measurable, and potentially useful. It may be that a sub-group living in Sierra Leone holds in their DNA immunity to diseases commonly suffered by those in Arizona. Or it may be that a common disability found in children in Sierra Leone has been completely eliminated by those living in Arizona, and by studying the differences between the groups and their development, we might be able to understand why, and what might be done to alleviate that problem worldwide.

Because of the aforementioned recent history of such research, however, it's difficult to have an untainted discussion about this field of inquiry. Discussing race has become a hot-button topic that, in polite company, and in parts of the world where we don't want to accidentally make any one group feel excluded or victimized, we'll sometimes avoid completely.

This is a good trend in some ways. I'm not of the opinion that the best way to use one's freedom of speech is to intentionally say hateful and hurtful things, and I'm not of the opinion that progressive scientific inquiry means we should run full-speed toward things we don't understand, unaware of or unbothered by the full spectrum of potential risks, including social ones.

That said, I also think we're leaving a lot of valuable information, especially cures and treatments, on the table. The best current understanding seems to be that, while race is a social construct—we say this color skin, this culture, this religion, all add up to "being Hispanic" or "being Nordic"— there are, in fact, differences in the genes we carry, and those genes are passed on through procreation. Procreation is regional by its very nature, so our genetic differences also tend to be carved up along cultural and geographic lines.

The social definition of race is what's killing us here, because on the genetic level, no one is "pure" anything. There are groups of people who have been almost completely isolated for generations who lack the full genetic diversity the rest of us now enjoy, but it's unusual. When we draw a line around someone and say, "They're Hispanic," we're making a social claim. To actually identify a person genetically, we'd need more than just a single word to do it; there's just too much variation to do otherwise. At the DNA level, we're all so utterly complex and unique the only label that comes close to capturing who we are is our own name.

If we could have a more complex discussion about this topic, I think we could establish that the links we draw between socially constructed racial identity and genetic identity are flawed and probably shouldn't correlate with each other. Unfortunately, that kind of conversation doesn't often happen. Our communication channels are increasingly primed for concise, surface-level bursts of chatter, which is beneficial in some ways, for some things, but crippling for everything else. Our attention spans have contracted accordingly, and although we now have more mediums of information exchange than ever before, which connect us with more people than ever before, the sorts of conversations we're able to have and the types of data we can easily distribute and discuss have constricted.

As a result, even though we understand a lot about the social and genetic facets of race, we have trouble discussing it. We're stuck in echo chambers, unaware of data that might make us open up and have more valuable conversations. We're also tucked away in warm, safe, information bubbles that help us feel secure in our own pre-held opinions, and which tell us anyone who disagrees with us is not just wrong, but outrageous.

How do we improve upon this? How do we have difficult conversations about topics steeped in emotion and traumatic historical precedent?

How do we talk about race in a productive setting? One in which everyone involved feels comfortable and empowered, but also one in which they can feel they're aiming for the same goals and don't need to trounce the opposition in order to win?

Part of the problem is we're taught that in every discussion there must be a winner and a loser. The most logical, fact-backed discussions tend to be debates, but these are often just quick-paced recitations of data, which fail to change minds, instead reshaping discussion as a sport in which you cheer for your own team. Maybe you appreciate the tactics the other side uses, but you never swap your jersey for one of theirs. It's a clash predicated on conflict, not a deep-dive to the root of the issue. It's about winning, not figuring out how everyone can win.

Trying to ensure everyone walks away a victor, to me, is a good starting point for any conversation. But making this happen requires an understanding of what we're really talking about when we enter a dialogue.

It's possible to have a discussion of race, for instance, and talk right past each other. One side uses the word "race" in the social context, and the other uses it to describe a collection of genetic components commonly found in a regional subgroup. If a scientist were to use the latter description in discussion with a sociologist using the former, she could very easily be construed as not just heartless, but perhaps even racist, while the sociologist might seem totally daft, as he'll be arguing about traits which aren't relevant to the conversation the scientist believes she's having.

We do this all the time within our interpersonal discussions. Maybe we have a throw down with our significant other about who washes the dishes and who never picks up after themselves, only to find, after an hour of shouting and tears, that the dishes, the laundry on the floor, wasn't the issue at all. The discussion we were really having was actually about how we each show we care, or the time we spend with each other, or the way we perceive expressions of love. Those other things were just tangible manifestations of what was churning beneath the surface.

If we're careful, we can recognize and address the actual causes of our flare-ups, or of potential, future explosions, before they become a serious issue. We can discuss both socially constructed race and scientifically relevant race, and we can do so in the same conversation. These are both important issues, and although one or the other will be more immediately relevant to some people, if we're able to sit down under the right circumstances and engage in a mutually trusting and respectful way, we stand a much better chance of achieving common understanding, each learning something we didn't know or comprehend before.

This situation requires a sense that the other person is not trying to harm you, within the context of the conversation or otherwise. It also requires you have a shared desire to arrive at conclusions and achieve solutions, rather than trying to "win" in the sense of out-arguing or out-shouting the other person. If one person wins and the other loses, both people have lost. A solo victory is a hollow one in this context because it means you have failed to make yourself understood, and you have failed to understand the other person.

This type of discussion can seem unlikely. It's not something our media, our news outlets, even our interpersonal conversations often produce on their own. We have debates, we have shouting matches on television between talking heads, we have isolated opinion pieces in newspapers, sometimes published side-by-side with an opposing viewpoint, both pieces failing to engage with the other or even recognize the legitimacy of the other's viewpoint. We're more likely to be served up opposition as entertainment than healthy, mature, mutually beneficial interactions between people who happen to disagree, because the latter is not good television, doesn't garner clicks, does not inspire outrage or the satisfaction of seeing your perceived team defeat a perceived Other.

This type of discussion can also be tricky to set up on a

smaller scale. I've been able to enjoy such conversations a few dozen times with a handful of different people, but each time it felt like we were exploring unfamiliar terrain. My conversation partner and I both experienced missteps along the way, accidentally using labels without defining them, taking offense when no offense was meant, and feeling under attack when asked to justify a statement we made about our beliefs.

Having a complete, complex, non-combative conversation is not easy. It requires, *in situ* with another person, you do a lot of personal exploration and learn something about yourself, your beliefs, and your biases. It requires you give ground, not just try to take it. It requires you feel good about giving that ground, seeing it as a victory not a defeat. It requires you set aside a lot of ego and become cognitively engaged with another person in a way that begins to feel almost intimate. You expose yourself psychologically and intellectually and they do the same. You trust the other person not to stab the weak spots you show them, and you, yourself, struggle against the urge to stab theirs during a moment of weakness.

I don't know if something like this could ever scale. Maybe it's a pipe dream to even try.

But maybe if enough of us want to have such conversations, we could have more of them and establish platforms and pre-built formats that would allow more people to join in. Could we convince a major news network to replace their shouting, angry, talking heads, endlessly repeating talking points at a camera with something more engaging, educational, and valuable?

Maybe, maybe not. But engaging in such conversations ourselves and acknowledging they're possible to begin with is a good place to start if we sincerely hope to become who we need to be.

Outro

We've all descended from bold survivalists and explorers.

It's thought our common genetic ancestors expanded outward from their geographic womb a mere 100,000 years ago. Which is a long time if we think in terms of a single lifespan, but a mere sliver of a splinter of a flake of time, if we think about the broader, deeper timeline.

On the scale of evolutionary biology, and on the scale of planetary development, and on the scale of galactic formation, measuring in hundreds of thousands of years is quaint. Barely worth mentioning. And yet we've done so much in such a short period of time.

This is heartening to me.

I like that every single human being alive today is descended from incredibly resilient, competitive stock, which was handed off securely through the years by those who lived to those who would live. Each historical step toward where we are today, even if mundane in the moment, a forgotten act by a forgotten person, was meaningful. These steps brought us here, together. Our forebears provided us with the bedrock of modernity, and gave us as many tools as could be mustered with the knowledge of their time to ensure we, too, would persevere. Would continue that rich tradition of not being able to leave things well enough alone, needing to know what's on the other side of that mountain range, and building something steady and supportive upon which the next generation can stand.

Looking at the world with an eye for possibilities helps us continue this uniquely human tradition of imagining and then making.

Recognizing the connections between seemingly disparate things helps us envision, invent, and understand cause and effect on a global scale.

Communicating clearly and with the proper intent allows us to organize and bring our collective will to bear against any challenge we might face.

Starting with ourselves—ensuring we're capable and stable, fulfilled and energized—is prudent if we want to participate in the broader swathe of activity swirling and pulsing all around us.

How we act, how we feel, how we treat each other determines the shape of our societies. Those societies, in turn, shape the future.

Few customs remain relevant and deserve maintenance after a hundred thousand years, but our species' historical practice of surviving, thriving, and making tomorrow better than today—I think—is a tradition worth retaining.

Acknowledgements

For an author, going through the editing process can feel like being beaten with a hammer, only to learn in the aftermath that you look better with bruises and fewer teeth.

* * *

A huge thanks to these skilled hammer-wielders:

Morgane Quilfen, Hilda-Christine Groenewald, Don Schulz, Jes Stevenson, Will Bricker, Willo Radgens, Bree Gaudette, Henry Wagner, Woodland Hunter, Lorien Goodale, Heather Moore, Kristine Asercion, Rui Ferreira, Joni Edison, Haley Lawrence, Carol Gunby, Sarah Oleinick, Jessica Constable, Teresa Remple, Laura Borem, Philipp Drehmann, Kat Tischler, and Eve Socarras.

About the Author

Colin Wright is a person who is learning in public.

He generally travels quite a lot, juggles many projects and interests, and is fortunate to have some wonderful people in his life.

Visit colin.io to learn more about Colin and/or peruse his books, podcasts, and other work.

www.ingramcontent.com/pod-product-compliance
Lightning Source LLC
Chambersburg PA
CBHW030821090426
42737CB00009B/820